GARDEN CITY MOVEMENT UP-TO-DATE

By EWART G. CULPIN

LONDON:
GARDEN CITIES & TOWN PLANNING ASSOCIATION,
3, GRAY'S INN PLACE, W.C.

1/- NET

THE GARDEN CITY MOVEMENT UP-TO-DATE

BY

EWART G. CULPIN

(Secretary to the Garden Cities and Town Planning Association)

THE GARDEN CITIES AND TOWN PLANNING ASSOCIATION
3, GRAY'S INN PLACE, LONDON, W.C.
1913

A PROPHET'S PLEA FOR GARDEN CITIES.

"As I sit at my work at home, which is at Hammersmith, close to the river, I often hear some of that ruffianism go past the window of which a good deal has been said in the papers of late, and has been said before at recurring periods. As I hear the yells and shrieks and all the degradation cast on the glorious tongue of Shakespeare and Milton, as I see the brutal, reckless faces and figures go past me, it rouses the recklessness and brutality in me also, and fierce wrath takes possession of me, till I remember that it was my good luck only of being born respectable and rich, that has put me on this side of the window among delightful books and lovely works of art, and not on the other side, in the empty street, the drink-steeped liquor-shops, the foul and degraded lodgings. I know by my own feelings and desires what these men want, what would have saved them from this lowest depth of savagery; employment which would foster their self-respect and win the praise and sympathy of their fellows, and dwellings which they could come to with pleasure, surroundings which would soothe and elevate them; reasonable labour, reasonable rest."

WILLIAM MORRIS, at Burslem, 1881.

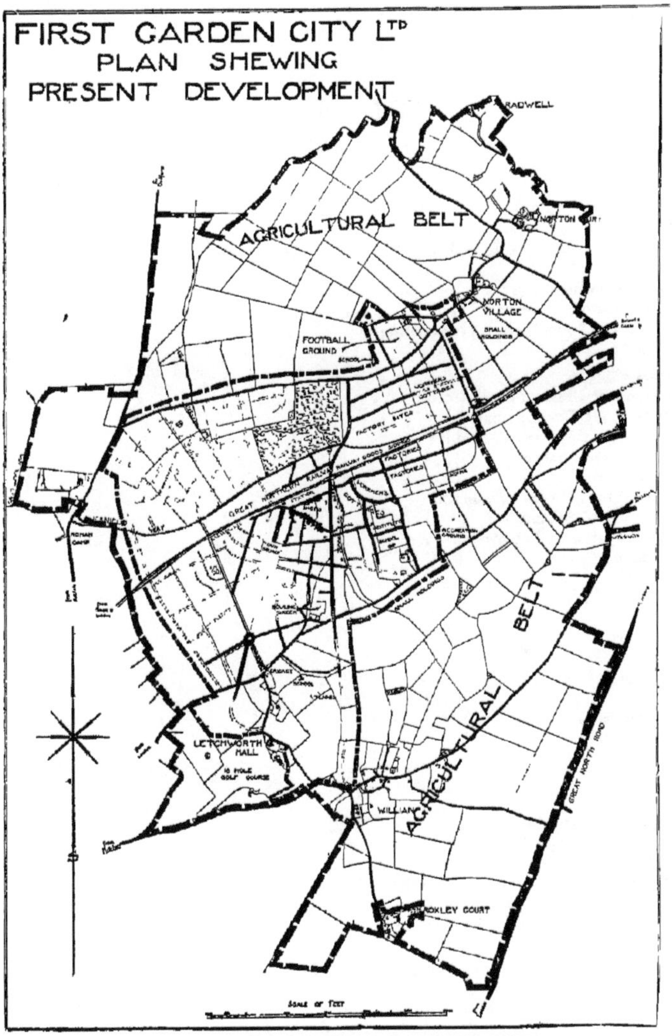

PLAN OF LETCHWORTH GARDEN CITY

This plan illustrates some of Mr. Ebenezer Howard's main proposals The whole area is 4,566 acres, of which the town area, shown by the broken line, occupies about 1,500 acres, the remainder forming the Agricultural Belt, which entirely surrounds the urban land The present population is 8,500, against some 400 souls who lived in the villages of Radwell, Norton, Letchworth, and Willian, the position of which is indicated above. The ultimate population provided for on the town area is 30,000, together with 5,000 on the agricultural belt.

CONTENTS.

Map showing developments on Garden City lines in Great Britain where a limitation of dividend is observed.

THE GARDEN CITY MOVEMENT UP-TO-DATE

1899—1914

WHEN fifteen years ago the Garden City Association was first formed, it was necessary in the literature that was published from time to time to point out in graphic form and detail the necessity for action along the lines which were advocated by Mr. Ebenezer Howard Thirteen years of propaganda have, however, brought home to the minds of the thinking part of the population the fact of the awful wastage that is going on through the ill-housing of the people, and through the haphazard growth of our centres of population Month by month the pages of GARDEN CITIES AND TOWN PLANNING, the organ of the Garden City and Town Planning Movement, has contained information shedding new light on the varied phases of this difficult question, and it may fairly be claimed that the knowledge of garden city principles has spread into every civilised nation under the sun There is, therefore, not the same necessity that there was to quote statistics to prove we are rearing in our slums an enfeebled rickety race, and that by our neglect a slum population is growing up which is foredoomed to degeneration The following particulars will, however, show graphically the effect upon health, and especially upon the health of the child, of life in the slums and life in a properly planned community

Since the first efforts of the Garden City Association, which followed upon the excellent work done at Bournville and Port Sunlight, numerous examples of garden suburb and garden village work have branched out in various parts of Great Britain, and an endeavour is here made to supply the salient facts relating to each It may be that some schemes are omitted, and it is hoped that, if this is the case, particulars will be forwarded for a succeeding issue. Every effort has been made to obtain the utmost degree of accuracy, and the figures given have been supplied by the companies or societies concerned

Although growing out of the garden city movement, not all of these ventures are upon the lines pursued by Mr. Ebenezer Howard in his original book "Garden Cities of To-morrow"; in fact, Letchworth is the only garden city in existence. Several garden suburbs and garden villages have grown up, while, in addition to this, there are quite a number of schemes which take the title "Garden City" promiscuously, without having any claim whatever to use the name, their objects being as foreign as possible to the conceptions of the founder of the movement

THE ESSENTIALS OF A GARDEN CITY.

It may be well to set out at the beginning the essentials of a garden city as distinguished from a garden suburb, and from ordinary development These may be stated as follows .—

1. That before a sod is cut, or a brick is laid, the town must in its broad outlines be properly planned with an eye to the convenience of the community as a whole, the preservation of natural beauties, the securing of the utmost degree of healthfulness, and proper regard to communication with the surrounding district.

2. That in the town area the number of houses to each acre should be strictly limited, so that every dwelling should have ample light and air, with a suitable garden, and that public recreation ground and open space should be provided generously

3 That the town area should for ever be surrounded by a belt of agricultural and park land, so that while in the centre the urban problem is being dealt with, the rural portion, which should be the larger part of the estate, may be available for farms and small holdings, in order that the small holder and market gardener may have a new market direct to hand for the sale of produce

4. That the return on capital should be limited to, say, 5 per cent, any profit above that amount being applied to the estate itself for the benefit of the community.

5 That the town should be not merely residential, but also commercial and industrial, that provision should exist for taking the worker and his work away from the crowded centres into the fresh air of the country district, where not only should the land be cheaply obtainable for the employer, but the worker should have a comfortable cottage at a convenient distance from his labour.

It is, therefore, essential that the land should be of considerable area, and its development should be in the hands of one controlling body, which, in Mr Howard's scheme, should have for its ultimate object, not the making of huge profits, but the improvement of the conditions of life for all who live on the area. The estate should be somewhere from six to ten square miles in area, and in order to give effect to the desire for the combination of town and country, about two-thirds should be reserved for the rural area.

CITIES, SUBURBS, AND VILLAGES.

In view of the many distorted ideas of what a Garden City is and the confusion which has resulted between Garden Cities, Garden Suburbs, and Garden Villages, it may be well to quote a succinct definition of the three phrases :—

A "Garden City" is a self-contained town, industrial, agricultural, residential—planned as a whole—and occupying land sufficient to provide garden-surrounded homes for at least 30,000 persons, as well as a wide belt of open fields. It combines the advantages of town and country, and prepares the way for a national movement, stemming the tide of the population now leaving the countryside and sweeping into our overcrowded cities

A "Garden Suburb" provides that the normal growth of existing cities shall be on healthy lines; and, when such cities are not already too large, such suburbs are most useful, and even in the case of overgrown London they may be, though on the other hand they tend to drive the country yet further afield, and do not deal with the root evil—rural depopulation

"Garden Villages," such as Bournville and Port Sunlight, are Garden Cities in miniature, but depend upon some neighbouring city for water, light and drainage; they have not the valuable provision of a protective belt, and are usually the centre of one great industry only

The Garden City therefore stands as the preventive, not as the palliative

There is general agreement that the housing of the people and the evil environment of that housing are very potent factors of our social maladies The aggregation of population is in itself an evil Wherever more than a certain number of people are housed on a given area of land, no matter whether they be in the best of "model dwellings," there the vital statistics show the progress of the evil.

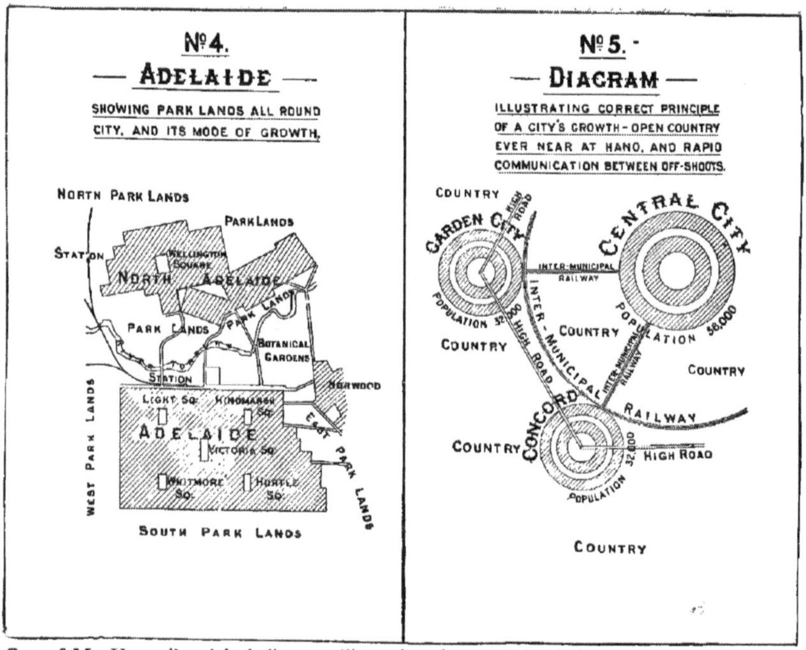

One of Mr. Howard's original diagrams illustrating the principle of the agricultural belt, and his suggestions for extension when the first Garden City has reached its limit of population.

Croft Lane, Letchworth, on the Agricultural Belt.

The central area of Letchworth, showing the new railway station and the shopping area.

Hillshott, Letchworth.

One of the problems most seriously affecting civilised humanity to-day is the twin problem of the overcrowding of the towns and the depopulation of the countryside Wherever we inquire, whether it be in the industrial countries of the old world or the more newly developed settlements of the new, the same state of things is to be found—everywhere the towns are becoming too large and, particularly noticeable in the old countries, the rural population is decreasing at such a rate as seriously to jeopardise the proper carrying on of husbandry.

TOWN AND COUNTRY—ADVANTAGES AND DISADVANTAGES.

The industrial revolution of the last century, while it led to much material advantage and greatly increased the financial prosperity of the country, was responsible for many evils, which, although not perceived at the time, are none the less pernicious in their results.

Fifty or sixty years ago the bulk of the population of this country lived in rural conditions, but it is estimated that at the present time six-sevenths is born and bred in large towns and cities. The growth of mechanical industries and the higher money wages which resulted, caused the rural dwellers to flock into the towns and to neglect the countryside, where at eighteen years of age a man was earning as much as he ever would earn as an agricultural labourer Too often country life presented a picture of helplessness and hopelessness; there was no opportunity for improved conditions of employment, for recreation, for education, or for social life Housing conditions presented features as horrible as the worst slum can show; sanitation, lighting, water, and the other services which the town-dweller has come to regard as a necessity are altogether lacking, and it is not to be wondered at that the lights of the town and its gold-paved streets have proved a fatal fascination to the hundreds of thousands who have come to swell the already overcrowded labour market

And the town, with all the advantages of commerce and high monetary wages, with education, amusement, and all the services of civilisation, has its dark underworld, whose real inwardness is hardly known to those whose lot is cast in more pleasant places. The march of science, the increasing activity of sanitary authorities, and the efficiency of their officials, backed by an enormous expenditure of money, has resulted in much improvement in the condition of our large cities, but still there is the slum and the overcrowding, still disease, dirt, and degradation And even where in their extreme these conditions do not prevail, we find dreariness, monotony, inconvenience, and absolute divorce from the beauties of nature: we are trying to breed an imperial race out of the material which makes for ruin and decay

A satisfactory solution of the problem thus presented must therefore go a long way towards the prevention of destitution. Anything which brings a new hope to humanity, any force which may be expended on creating a new condition of life, and any new economic truth which is capable of adaptation to the varying needs of the dwellers in town and in country, in old worlds and in new worlds, must be hailed as leading to that prophetic day and that ideal city which the dreamers of every age have dreamt of from the time of Isaiah down to William Morris.

THE FOUNDER.

As is the case with so many great movements, the Garden City idea was the outcome of the man of the people—unknown beyond his immediate circle, and without the resources of wealth and privilege to forward his project. It is not too much to say that Mr. Ebenezer Howard, the founder of the Garden City movement, will be remembered in history when the names of many prominent politicians and soldiers have been forgotten, for of him alone can it be said in modern times that he founded a city, and not only founded one city but that by his practical enthusiasm and his clear-sighted idealism he gave to the world an idea which has resulted in a few years in a complete change of the ordinary methods of town extension and estate development It was only in 1898 that, after studying for many years the social problems of the country, and observing the results which had come with the improved environment of the people, he published a book called "To-morrow: A Peaceful Path to Real Reform," subsequently issued as "Garden Cities of To-morrow."

The problem which Mr Ebenezer Howard set himself out to solve was to show that by starting entirely new towns in rural districts, free from the vicious inheritance of generations of town life and slum degeneracy, an opportunity would be given for a fuller, freer, life, and that the mental, moral, and intellectual development would follow as surely as the physical. It was not an easy problem, although it is so much taken for granted nowadays It was really the creation of new economic conditions. First, it involved town planning, then quite a new idea in this country, but through Mr. Howard's initial work and the labours of those who gathered round him, now an accepted necessity and embodied in an Act of Parliament

Before a sod was cut or a brick was laid, in its main outlines at least, the new city must take its form upon paper. By so doing, traffic difficulties would be avoided in the future By the proper restriction of areas, schemes of lighting, drainage, and water supply could be planned out from the beginning, with no uncertainty as to the whereabouts of the future population The limitation of the number of houses was an essential point, in many districts to-day the municipal by-laws allow fifty-six and even sixty houses to be crowded on to an acre of land, giving a population, even in cottage property, of some three hundred people to the acre, while in tenement dwellings the number comes up still higher.

Profiting by investigations that have been made by scientists, a limit of twelve houses to the net acre was determined upon, and this, with the provision of ample open spaces, parks, and recreation grounds, and allowing for generous grass-lined roadways, will mean on the average of five people to a house, no greater population than thirty people to the acre.

But it was not enough to plan where the town should grow, it was necessary to say where it should stop It is being borne in upon the minds of thinkers that our big towns are too big, and that where you go along adding village to town and town to city, so that you have huge conglomerations like London—or, as in south-east Lancashire, practically one great town twenty-five or thirty miles long and eight or ten miles wide—and where your population is numbered by the hundred thousand, you have practically shut out the benefits of fresh air and pure sunlight from the great mass of the dwellers The idea, therefore, in creating garden cities is to aim at towns with populations of between thirty thousand, lower than which it would not be possible to go to enable the necessary provisions to be made, and sixty or seventy thousand, beyond which access to the countryside begins to be in danger.

THE INDUSTRIAL ASPECT.

To secure the proper restriction of the town, Mr. Howard conceived the idea of the agricultural belt of land encircling the town area and providing upon its farms and small holdings an opportunity for the solution there of rural problems, while in the town area urban questions were being settled

But it was useless to talk about fresh air and sunlight to the man who has to earn his daily bread by the sweat of his brow, unless you give him an opportunity of continuing his employment This meant the provision of work near to his home.

Few people have realised the enormous economic waste involved in carrying work people to and from their work. Not only is much time wasted, but the conditions of workmen's trains are such that serious physical results must follow, and we are probably thereby laying up a store of nervous disorders.

But apart from that, with improved forms of transit, it is not necessary for mechanical industries all to be carried on at one centre, and all in big towns. Years before the Garden City movement came to birth individual manufacturers were finding that it paid them to take their works out into the country districts, where the cheapness of land and the lower expenditure on rates, etc., amply repaid them for their outlay. It is true there were failures, and there have been failures since then, but this is where the Garden City movement met the problem and solved it by organising the migration of manufacturers. Only the largest firms could provide housing, sewerage, water, gas, and other facilities for their work-people, and the failures were deterring further experiments when Mr. Howard showed how, under the Garden City scheme, the combination of manufacturers in conjunction with residential development, could do what was not possible to individuals. The cheapness of land enabled factories to be built all on one floor, and with proper lighting; it enabled cottages to be built cheaply and reasonably near the factories; and it also provided that each house should have an ample amount of garden ground around it. Working in a London factory often means living in a slum, with the children's playground in the gutter, or on the stairs of a "model dwelling"; it means an exorbitant rent in the centre, and if the worker lives in the suburbs what he saves on rent he spends on railway fare.

The financial side of the question was given very careful thought and study, because it was realised from the beginning that even if sufficient money could be found to equip such a venture at the start, unless it could be proved a commercial success, no one else would be likely to make the experiment, and it would be impossible to impress upon the country, and upon the State, the value of development upon these lines. In order to adjust the claims of capital and of production it was proposed that the dividend on capital should be limited to 5 per cent., and that all profits above this sum should be devoted to the benefit of the community. The land would be bought as a whole at agricultural prices, and a freehold retained by the company. As the population increased, so would the value go up, and this value would be for the benefit of the people themselves. The developing company was to act as a sort of trustee, and when the estate was sufficiently advanced to run on its own legs it was hoped that it would be possible to hand over the whole concern to some body which should act as permanent trustees for the community at the original price which had been paid for the estate, which should henceforth be carried on in the interests of the dwellers on the spot.

The promulgation of these principles thirteen years ago was received with that kindly cynicism with which most changes are greeted. "Utopian," "beautiful but impracticable," "wildly visionary," and many another epithet is found on looking through the newspaper press of that day. Except in a few quarters, the scheme was hailed as idyllic; few deemed it possible of success. But the few have proved the truer prophets.

THE WORK OF THE GARDEN CITY ASSOCIATION.

After a few years' propagandist work by the Garden City Association (now the Garden Cities and Town Planning Association), which was called into being to foster the new idea, a pioneer company was formed to make investigations, and in 1903 First Garden City Ltd. was formed to develop the estate of nearly four thousand acres at Letchworth. Here many of Mr. Howard's original ideas have been put into practice, modified, of course, by the

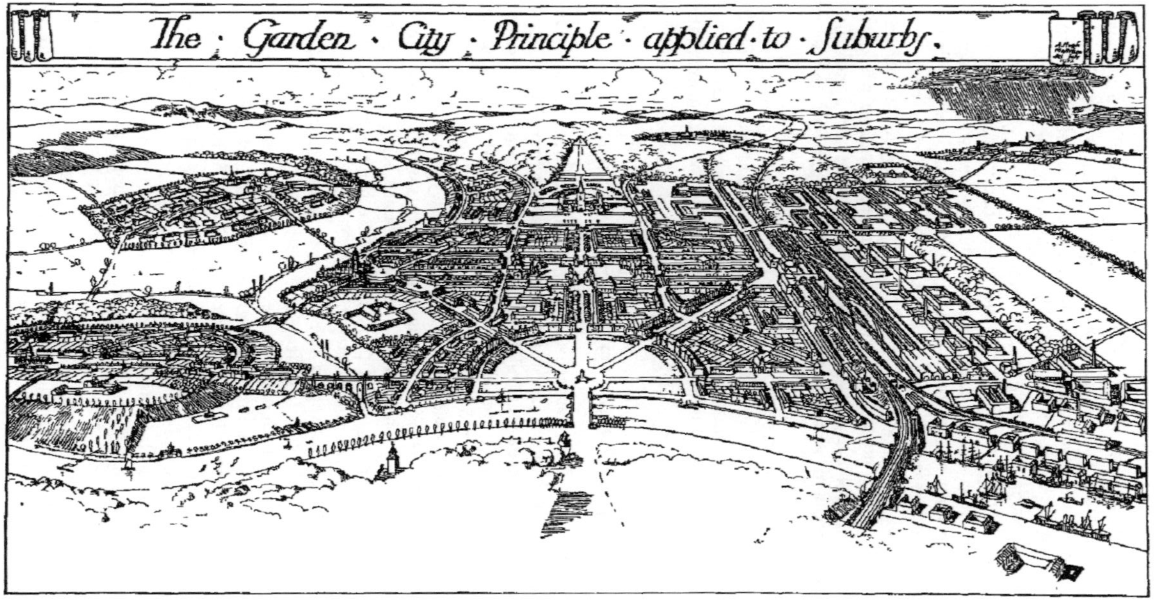

Mr Raymond Unwin here illustrates the application of the Garden City principle of a belt of green encircling the whole community to the extension of new Suburbs. The Suburbs are seen separated from the city by belts of land, which will remain open for all time.

requirements of the site, and hindered oftentimes by the lack of sufficient capital; but yet being pressed onwards by men with an ample faith in the soundness of the project and in the ultimate realisation of triumphant success That success has now been achieved What a few years ago was arable and pasture land with a scattered population of a few score people is now a thriving industrial and residential centre with a population of some seven thousand people, which is being added to day by day, as the requirements of those desiring to live there are met by the provision of additional cottages.

It was not long before it was seen that this movement had in it a much wider application than the building of new towns That was the ideal; that was the solution of the problem. It would keep men on the land, and bring others back to the land It was grand; it was heroic, but it was very hard And not everywhere were conditions suitable. Our great towns were still growing, and in the nature of things they must continue to grow. Despite the knowledge that this meant the increasing shutting out of nature, and although it would not be possible on the margins of our towns to provide the agricultural belt or the provision for factories and workers, at least the other parts of the scheme were applicable

Why should our suburbs grow in streets of endless monotony, of absolute lack of beauty? The complete segregation of classes was not good, the absence of local centres destroyed local patriotism, homes become dormitories, and the garden—where it had not become a rubbish heap—was the show ground of weakly exotics, whose too frequent libations were hastening them to an untimely end.

THE GROWTH OF THE GARDEN SUBURB.

With characteristic energy Mrs. Barnett took up the Garden Suburb idea There was a scheme for the enlargement of Hampstead Heath, and she saw an opportunity of combining this preservation of a beautiful piece of nature's handiwork and an attempt to weave into man's work some threads of nature's How well she has succeeded need hardly be told From the opening, in 1907, the original area of 240 acres has already been dealt with, and further extensions have been purchased The population has increased to 4,500, and, by the exercising of judicious control, a community has been brought into being which is the mecca of the architect all over the world. Many subsidiary experiments are being tried there, and the example so given has encouraged scores of people elsewhere to take similar steps, with a consequence that to-day there are some forty Garden Suburb and Village schemes in existence in this country, all embracing in one degree or another principles which were enunciated by the founder of the Garden City movement.

So far, the second Garden City has yet to be built The Garden Suburb has not to create new conditions, but simply to direct an existing flow, and, therefore, since we as a people are inclined to take the line of least resistance, the Garden Suburb succeeds the more quickly. The child has outstripped the parent, and in some degree the great truth has been in danger of becoming overshadowed by the lesser truth.

The Garden Cities and Town Planning Association does not for one moment discourage Garden Suburbs. It has helped in the formation of several, and hopes to continue that work, being engaged week in and week out in preaching the advantages of the principle. But that does not mean that we have lost sight of the fact that the true solution is in the Garden City. For the extension of that principle we shall continue to work, side by side with encouraging the growth of the Suburbs. The big landowners are coming to our aid; in all parts of the country tracts of land are being properly planned by men who have had their training in our Association's work, and areas which might have been covered with unlovely dwellings are being laid out with every regard to decency and order.

Finally, the municipalities are now awaking and joining in the march onward. The Housing, Town Planning, etc., Act of 1909 gives them powers to do what the Garden City has already done, and in this connection it is interesting to read the prophetic words of one of our leading newspapers. In speaking of the growth of the movement some six or eight years ago, it said "The Garden City pioneers have shown the way Private enterprise, as it usually does in this country, has given an example to the State" The State has followed the example; and although no voice of statesmen has been uplifted to sing his praises, there is no man more responsible for the acceptation of town planning principles in this country than was Mr Ebenezer Howard. When many of to-day's advocates of town planning were dumb and ignorant, he preached its merits More, he secured its application; and if a future England sees its towns grow up more healthily, more beautiful, more convenient, more than to any other one man will they owe that fact to the humble pioneer of Garden City principles.

The following details of schemes have been collected with a view to including eventually all housing schemes which have a claim to notice, and therefore others than those on Garden City lines have been inserted. In the table which follows will be found full particulars of the character of these, as far as they can be obtained Even after months of endeavour many details are lacking, but it is hoped that the attempt to include for the first time some account of the chief English housing experiments in one booklet will find its reward in producing something which shall be of service to all studying the movement

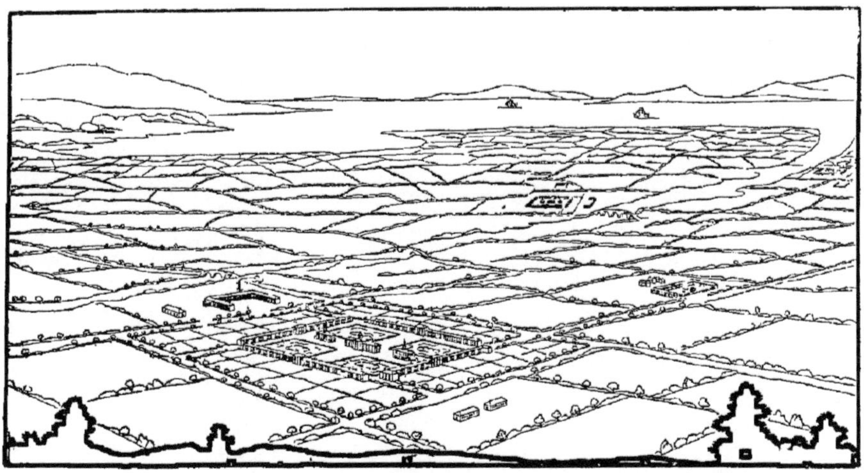

Robert Owen's scheme for a model town "Harmony," from his own description published in 1817

SUMMARY OF THE PRESENT POSITION OF THOSE ESTATES AND SOCIETIES OF WHICH PARTICULARS ARE AVAILABLE

Name of Estate	Total area (in acres)	Now developed	How Controlled †	Dividend limited to	Share Capital Authorised	Share Capital Issued	Local Rates	Operations began	Present Number of Houses	Present population	Houses per acre	Ultimate Houses expected	Ultimate Population	Minimum Rents	
Alkrington	700	10	D	—	—	—	—	1911	40	170	17	8,400	30,000	6/6	
Anchor Tenants (Leicester)	48	15	E	5 %	—	£2,38-	4/8	Sept., 1907	94	360	10	250	1,250	6/ †	
Blackley	243	9	(Municipal)	—	—	—	8/1	1901	150	600	17	2,810	11,240	6/4†	
Bournville	609	138	C	(see particulars)			7/4	1879	920	4,390	6	3,654	15,000	5/-	
Bournville Tenants	20	20	E	5 %	£10,664	£10,664	—	Aug 1906	146	750	11	146	750	6/-†	£35
Bristol	26	7	A	5 %	£10,000	£3,781	—	1909	44	178	14	280	1,400	6/6	
Caerphilly	10	—	E	5 %	—	—	—	1913	24	120	10	100	500	5/6	
Coventry	14	2	E	5 %	-	£1,660	8/3	Oct., 1912	12	40	14	189	945	6/6†	
Cuffley	350	-	B	—	—	—	5/6	1913	—	—	5	2,750	10,000	7/6	
Datchet	30	30	E	5 %	—	—	—	1913	—	—	10	—	—	10/6	
Derwentwater Tenants	2½	2½	E	5 %	—	£1,054	6/	Oct., 1909	2	8[illegible]	12	27	135	5/6	
Didsbury	7	2	I	5 %	£1 300	—	8/2	Mar., 1907	30	102	15*	30	102	7/6	
Ealing	63	40	F	5 %	—	£27,498	6/8	April, 1901	510	2,000	12	700	3,500	6/6	£57
Fairfield Tenants	25	—	L	5 %	—	—	—	Dec., 1912	—	—	12	270	1,080	5/-	
Fallings Park	400	8½	D & E	—	—	—	9/4	June, 1907	75	310	12	1 000	1,750	4/6†	
Garden City Tenants	F 39	39	E	5 %	—	£20,588	4/9	April, 1905	322	1,600	12*	322	1,600	4/6	
Gidea Park	500	108	D	—	£80,000	—	8/	May, 1910	188	700	8	4,000	16,000	11/6	
Glasgow	200	5	A	5 %	£25,000	£3,970	—	Oct., 1912	40	140	12	2,600	10,000	6/11	
Guildford	20	3½	D	—	—	—	—	Oct., 1910	32	—		160	650	7/6†	
Hadleigh	7	—	E	5 %	—	—	—	1913	—	—	—	—	—	4/3†	
Hampden Park	9	9	E	5 %	—	—	—	1909	73	—	11	98	450	8/6†	
Hampstead Garden Suburb	652	180	A	5 %	£75,000	£54,111	5/6	May, 1907	1 550	5 000	8*	2,000	—	5/9	
Hampstead Heath Extension Tenants	—	—	E	5 %	—	£10 700	5/6	July 1912	—	—	—	-	—	—	
Hampstead Tenants	F 27	27	F	5 %		£26,500	5/6	May 1907	271§	1,200	10*	271	1,200	6/-	
Harborne	54	54	E	5 %	—	£8 461	8/2	Sept., 1907	499	1 600	9.25	499	1,600	4/-†	
Haslemere	5 09	2	E	5 %	—	—	7/8	Mar 1912	20	80	10	60	200	6/4†	
Hereford	8 75	8 75	(see particulars)				—	1909	86	430	10	86	430	4/9†	
Hull	94	70	C	3 %	—	—	10/1	Nov., 1907	560	2,000	12	700	3,500	4/9†	
Ilford	40	20	A	5 %	—	—	8/6	Dec., 1909	70	200	8*	150	750	£30	
Knebworth	800	—	D	—	—	—	4/6	1909	250	1,250	8	6,400	19,000	5/6	
Llanidloes	9	—	A & E	5 %	—	—	7/6	June 1913	—	—	12	60	[illegible]	4/	
Letchworth (Garden City)	4,566	800	A	5 %	£300,000	£176,921	5/0	Sept., 1903	1 876	8,200	12*	7,000	35,000	4/3†	
Liverpool	180	25½	E	5 %	—	£39,500	8/6	July, 1910	260	1,000	12	1 800	7,000	7/-|	
Machynlleth	15	-	A & E	5 %	—	—	8/2	June, 1913	—	—	12	150	600	4/-	
Manchester (Burnage)	11	11	E	5 %	—	£6 722	8/4	1908	136	500	12	136	500	5/3	
Merthyr	17½	—	E	5 %	—	—	—	1913	32	—	—	175	875	6/6†	
New Earswick	120	39	C	(see particulars)			—	Dec., 1904	150	750	10	1,200	6,000	4/6	
New Eltham	27	—	E	5 %	—	--	—	May, 1913	—	—	11	—	1,400	7/6	
Oakwood Tenants	—	—	E	5 %	—	£6,450	5/6	Jan., 1913	100	420	—	-	—	7/-	
Oldham Garden Suburb	32½	17½	E	5 %	-	£11,271	8/8	1907	150	750	14	700	3 500	5/11	
Otford	160	—	E	5 %	—	—	.	1913	13	—	—	—	—	—	
Petersfield	32	—	E	5 %	—	—	—	1913	—	—	—	28	—	—	
Port Sunlight (a)	223	135	D	(see particulars)			—	1895	823	3,600	10	1,200	5,000	5/3†	
Rothley	1,000	150	D	—	—	—	5/9	1909	69	240	—	-	—	4/6†	
Rhubina	110	—	E	5 %	-	—	—	July, 1913	34	—	12	1 200	6,000	5/	
Ruislip Manor	1,300	100	A	5 %	£75,000	£30,000	7/4	April, 1911	100	300	12	5,000	20,000	5/	
Sealand	47	10	E	5 %	—	£5,150	1/10	July, 1910	108	550	10	470	2,500	1/9	
Second Hampstead Tenants	F 39	39	E	5 %		£59,970	5/6	Aug., 1909	377	1,900	10*	377	1,900	5/9	
Sevenoaks	6½	6½	E	5 %	£40,000	£2,555	6/2	1904	80	250	13	80	250	4/9	
Somersham	17½	—	E	5 %	£20,000	£475	—	1913	6	—	—	20	—	4/ †	
Stirling Homesteads	40	1½	F	5 %	—	£415	2/6	May, 1910	11	39	6	40	200	4/-	
Stoke-on-Trent	38½	13	E	5 %	—	£1,890	10/-	April, 1910	9	300	12	412	2,000	5/-	
Sutton (Surrey)	25½	—	E	5 %	—	£1,584	6/5	Feb., 1913	31	18	10	226	1 130	7/-	
Warrington (Great Sankey)	20	— }	A	5 %	£20,000	{ —	—	July, 1907	24	100	12	243	1,200 }	6/-†	
" (Grappenhall)	22	— }					—	July, 1907	12	55	12	260	1,300 }		
Woking	9	3	E	—	—	—	—	1912	21	—	8	72	350	4/-†	
Woodlands	127	127	(owned by Colliery Co.)				—	June, 1907	653	3,600	5 2	653	3,600	5/3†	
Wrexham	200	—	A & E	5 %	—	—	6/-	May, 1913	—	—	12	2,000	10,000	4/9	

A Public company limited dividend B Public company unlimited dividend C Trust D Owned privately
F Society of Public Utility under Provident Societies Act (a) Not including works area
F Not separate estates Area included in parent schemes

* Excluding roads etc. † Including rates
§ Blocks of shops and residential flats have also been erected
¶ A number of estates recently started have not yet made sufficient progress to warrant inclusion here Reference to most of these will be found on other pages

INTRODUCTION TO SECOND EDITION

PHENOMENAL GROWTH IN 1913.

THE first issue of the record of a great movement was almost necessarily incomplete in many details It was found difficult to obtain particulars of some estates, owing to the apathy of those in charge, and there are still omissions from the present edition

Even in the few months that have elapsed since the first issue was printed there is great progress to record, and information is given of no less than fifty additional ventures. As well as mentioning schemes not previously brought within the book, an attempt is made to give more adequate information regarding the pioneer schemes A new element is introduced by the application of co-partnership methods to rural housing, and details are given of what has been already done in this direction A further section deals with the progress of Town Planning under the Act of 1909.

In the past nine months the Garden City movement seems more than ever to have come into its own. The activity in every branch is remarkable, despite adverse conditions in regard to the building trade and an increasing tightness of money Large additions have been made to the number of new schemes now on foot. Many of the schemes that are called Garden City schemes have nothing in common with the Garden City movement but the name, which they have dishonestly appropriated Schemes of the wildest speculation, land-sweating, and jerry-building, have all been promoted in the hope that the good name would carry them through, but through the activity of the Association and through the growing knowledge of what Garden City development really means, as a rule these schemes have been countered, and their attempt to exploit the movement has sometimes been attended with financial disaster to themselves.

The educative work which has been done by the Garden Cities and Town Planning Association has spread far beyond what was at first thought to be its borders. Lectures are being given everywhere; literature is being supplied by thousands of copies, the monthly magazine, *Garden Cities and Town Planning*, is acquiring a firmer hold and obtaining a wider circulation, being recognised as the chief educative factor in civic improvement published in this country Scores of landowners have consulted the Association in regard to land which they are developing, and although the Garden City scheme may not be followed out in its entirety, there is the satisfaction of knowing that thousands of acres are being developed upon better lines than there was a probability of securing beforehand, and instead of the countryside being defaced by a repetition of the abominations that have been perpetrated around many of our large towns—and indeed in many of the small ones

—decent, comfortable cottages have been erected at a reasonable rental, serving not only to house the people who live in them but providing an example for the whole neighbourhood.

A WORLD-WIDE RECOGNITION.

There is not a portion of the civilised world to which the Garden City message is not now being sent regularly A return has just been made of correspondence dealt with in a period of two months, and this shows that the following countries have applied for information and particulars regarding the growth of the Garden City movement in England: The United States, Austria, France, Holland, Russia, Germany, South Africa, Poland, Belgium, Canada, New Zealand, India, Hungary, Roumania, New South Wales, Queensland, South Australia, West Australia, Victoria, Tasmania, Turkey, Norway, Sweden, Spain, Italy, Nova Scotia, Argentina, South Africa, Switzerland, Crete, Trinidad, Burma, Denmark, Japan, Ceylon, Uruguay, Greece, Fiji Islands, West Africa, Newfoundland, Egypt The names are taken haphazard from the list, and with no idea of order. In each of these countries are members of the Association, and the monthly magazine goes there regularly.

In many cases definite results have been accomplished in the formation of allied bodies in different parts of the world; elsewhere Town Planning schemes have been forwarded, or, again, model villages have been founded on co-partnership lines. Everywhere this message of the Garden City has been hailed with acclamation by men and women by whom the existing state of affairs is seen to be not only ugliness and inconvenience, but degradation —the loss of the love of the beautiful things of earth, the obsession of the human mind with the things that are really of little value, and the neglect of the great and overwhelming problems of existence.

A FORECAST.

There is much yet to be done before the Garden City movement can really be said to enter into full recognition. Garden Suburbs we can get in abundance, in five years' time the town that has not got a Garden Suburb will be an exception, and there will grow the tendency of surrounding the great centres of population with belts of houses built in reasonable surroundings; but still there will remain the great problem of the housing of the man in the middle of the town and the man at the bottom of the ladder

Improved sanitation will lessen the evils of the old centres, and the progress of humanitarianism in legislation will probably relieve some of the hardships of the very poorest, but after all that has been done and said, it does not seem feasible, under present conditions, to house the lowest-paid workers in decent houses at an economic price which they can afford to pay

It is hinted that great legislative changes are about to be proposed which will cheapen the cost of providing houses Cheap money and cheap land are promised, and these together may do something to bring down costs, and Town Planning will probably result in the establishment of many settlements having much the same physical appearance as have our Garden Suburbs But greater good would come to a greater number of people if there were only available funds to establish new Garden Cities, where the worker and his work can be out of the crowded centres and yet have all the advantages of the town in common with the delights of his garden.

LOST OPPORTUNITIES.

An opportunity of providing a world example is, alas! being lost through the Admiralty's attitude in regard to the proposal to create a model town at the new naval

Base at Rosyth, and the extraordinary improvidence of the Port of London Authority as to its responsibilities for the people who will have to live in the neighbourhood of the new Docks is not encouraging for those who look in high quarters for help in these matters

THE HOPE OF THE FUTURE—GARDEN CITIES.

It is in the working out of the complete scheme proposed by Mr. Howard that real progress seems to lie. At present about fifteen thousand acres are included in the area of the proposals of one sort and another enumerated in the following pages, and practically one-third of this area is at Letchworth If all this land were built upon to the modest extent expected, a population of some nine hundred thousand people would be housed on garden city lines, but at the present time about forty-five thousand are so housed, or a thousandth part of the population.

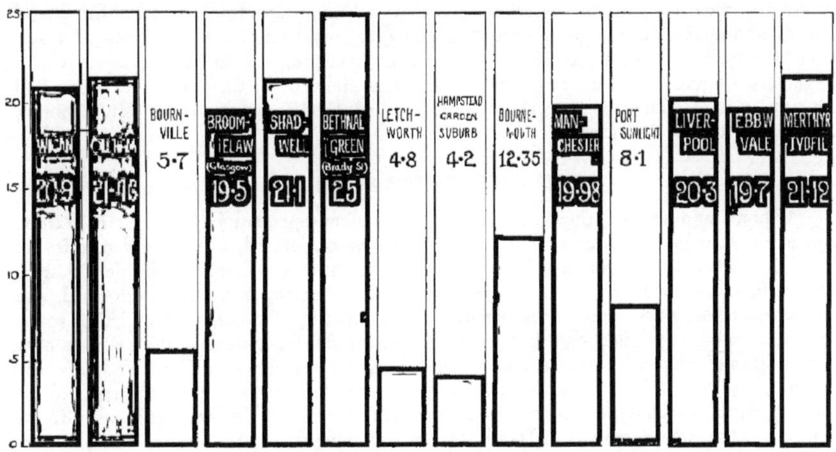

LIFE AND DEATH—THE TRIUMPH OF THE GARDEN CITY AND SUBURBS.

With the enormous improvement in traffic facilities, and the growing tendency to remove factories from town to country, the organised decentralisation of industry becomes less difficult, and as the experience of the pioneers becomes more widely known, the demand for real Garden Cities is likely to spread rapidly. The fact that better conditions of work mean better work, and that better conditions of life mean healthier and happier families, must have its influence, and the multiplication of Garden Cities will afford the best opportunity for clearing out the old slums and recreating that type of man which books and songs tell us of, but which modern town life has gone so far to destroy

THE INTERNATIONAL ASSOCIATION.

No survey of the movement would be complete unless it included an account of the work in other countries. A summary is therefore given of what has been done abroad. It will be seen that by far the most active progress has been made by the German Garden City Association The steady and persistent work of its official leaders has resulted in a knowledge of Garden City principles being spread throughout the whole empire, and the amount of useful instructive literature which has been issued by the German Association is equal in bulk and variety to that of the parent organisation

Shortly it should be possible to record the progress in America and Canada The three months I have recently spent in the United States and Canada convinces me that there is a great future there for the Garden City movement. The people are ready for such a movement, which attempts to solve problems that are pressing upon them more and more heavily as time goes on Where land speculation is threatening to ruin the whole community, the Garden City movement would come in with a message of hope for those who are striving to provide decent housing accommodation at a reasonable rent

These world-wide recognitions of the value of Mr Howard's proposals have accumulated in an extraordinary manner of late, and there has been evidenced a general desire that the various bodies which are striving towards the improvement of the civic ideal should be linked up with one another To this end an International Garden Cities and Town Planning Association has been formed with every prospect of a useful career Already some twenty nationalities are represented and the first congress, to be held next year in England, will give some idea of the extent to which the Garden City ideal has permeated the mind of man The new Association has done itself the honour of electing Mr Ebenezer Howard as its first President

THE CITY OF THE FUTURE.

At home and abroad, therefore, we find every encouragement for progress in Garden City work. The labour of the propagandist is not always requited, and it is given to few to see of the travail of their soul and be satisfied, but to those who labour in this field there is an ever-increasing pleasure in the honour so generously bestowed upon Mr. Howard, and the success of his work, even in the partial and fragmentary manner in which it has so far been attempted, is an incentive to secure wider and fuller recognition We see now only dim outlines of what the future town will be. We know it will not be like that death-trap which civilisation has created in the last fifty years, and it is just as unlikely to attain to the state of Arcadian bliss as pictured in *News from Nowhere* We are awaiting still the dawning of that new earth which Isaiah foresaw many years ago, and the woes and horrors of the dark side of town life are apt to make us forget, as we ponder over the problems which confront us, that there is a way out Years of educational work will have still to be spent, and the folly of tinkering with the evil must be taught to governments and peoples until they are prepared to do as was done at Letchworth—make a clean start. The city of the future will have a new meaning, for it will be a city of homes, and if the garden city idea—improved and perfected as newer conceptions arise—is kept in the forefront of men's vision, and not allowed to be hidden by easier methods of palliation which are not remedies, then they who work to-day will have laid well and truly a foundation upon which shall be reared a City of Hope, worthy of the dreams and hopes of prophets and reformers of all ages, —"and they shall bring the glory and honour of the nations into it"

THE STAGES OF PROGRESS.

The Garden City movement may be described as a modern miracle, and a direct contradiction of the dictum, "A prophet is not without honour, save in his own country" Whereas in many fields of social reform men have toiled and died without recognition, in less than a generation the Garden City movement has attained to a place of supreme importance throughout the world, and its founder has been hailed as one of the greatest men of his generation. Glancing through the pages which follow, it is difficult to realise that it was only in the year 1898 that Mr. Ebenezer Howard gave to the world his book entitled *To-morrow—a Peaceful Path to Real Reform*, afterwards issued as *Garden Cities of To-morrow*, which has practically changed the method of development in this and other countries, and which was the beginning here of the new science of town building which led to the passing of the Housing, Town Planning, etc., Act of 1909.

This was not the first that had been heard of the idea For years Mr. Howard had occupied all the spare time he could snatch from his busy life as an official shorthand writer in lecturing and writing upon the subject which was nearest his heart After the book had been published a number of sympathisers gathered around him, and on June 10th, 1899, formed the Garden City Association for the purpose of studying his proposals and considering their practical application.

IN 1899.

As illustrating the growth of the movement and the many ways in which Mr. Howard's ideas have been adapted, it is of interest to chronicle the changes in the "Objects" of this Association as shown in its rules The first statement ran as follows: "Objects. To promote the discussion of the project suggested by Mr. Ebenezer Howard in *To-Morrow*, and ultimately to formulate a practical scheme on the lines of that project, with such modifications as may appear desirable."

IN 1902.

In January, 1902, the objects appeared thus.—

"(*a*) To promote discussion of the project suggested by Mr Ebenezer Howard in his book *To-morrow*"

"(*b*) To take the initial step towards the formation in Great Britain, either by public company or otherwise, of Garden Cities, wherein shall be found the maximum attainable of comfort and convenience to the inhabitants, who shall themselves become, in a corporate capacity, the owners of the site, subject to the fullest recognition of individual as well as mutual and public interests"

In the Fourth Annual Report, for the year ending October 31st, 1902, these Objects are extended into a statement headed "Our Objects" and signed by the Chairman of the Council, Mr Ralph Neville, K.C., now the President, the Hon. Sir Ralph Neville This statement reads as follows —

"The exodus of the people from the country and the consequent overcrowding in the towns, with its attendant physical and moral evils, occupies the attention of all who are interested in social welfare.

"This Association has been formed to give practical effect to a scheme which attempts to deal with the question of 'How to get the people back to the land?'

"The idea is to bring the town to the country by the establishment of Industrial Centres in rural districts Successful experiments in this direction have already been carried out by Messrs. Cadbury at Bournville, near Birmingham, and Messrs. Lever at Port Sunlight, near Liverpool

"The outlines of the scheme are as follows —

"The purchase of land at agricultural prices; the laying-out of a town, section by section, upon the central portion of the estate, the remainder to be permanently retained for agricultural purposes. The necessary capital would receive a fixed return, and the balance of the increment in value would be applied for the benefit of the community in affording means of transit, etc.

"It is calculated that upon an estate of 6,000 acres one-sixth would suffice for the accommodation of a population of 33,000 people, and that the ground rents would provide for interest at the rate of £4 per cent per annum on the capital, and leave a large surplus.

"We claim for our proposals.—

1. That they recognise the impossibility of diverting labour by artificial means from the industries to which it flows by the natural operation of economic law.
2. That they bring the producer and consumer of agricultural produce into contact.
3. That the scheme has a sound financial basis resting upon the increase in the value of land caused by an influx of population.
4. That the economies in regard to construction, supply of power, transit, etc, resulting from the construction of a town in conformity with a predetermined plan, are great.
5. That no economic law is infringed, and no industry interfered with. If the scheme can be carried out, the ultimate benefit to the population of this country would be great. If it fails, the loss will be measured by the difference between the purchase and sale price of the estate and the cost of partly laying out a single section of the proposed town.

"The immediate object of the Association is to secure the attention of the public to their proposals, with the view of putting them to a practical test. The first practical step has been taken, and the Garden City Pioneer Company Limited, with a subscribed capital of £20,000, has been formed to investigate and negotiate with manufacturers.

"It is hoped that those who view with concern the shifting of our population from country to town will give the scheme of the Association their attention, and, if they approve, their countenance and support."

IN 1903.

At a special general meeting held at Essex Hall on July 9th, 1903, the objects were approved as follows:—

"To promote the relief of overcrowded and congested areas, to secure a wider distribution of the population over the land, and to advance the moral, intellectual, and physical development of the people by—

"(*a*) Taking initial steps to establish Garden Cities in which the inhabitants shall become in a corporate capacity the owners of the sites, subject to the fullest recognition of individual as well as public interest;

"(*b*) Encouraging the tendency of manufacturers and others to move from crowded centres to rural districts, co-operating with such manufacturers and with public bodies in securing healthy housing accommodation for the workpeople in proximity to their places of employment;

"(*c*) Co-operating with other organisations in promoting legislation to enlarge the powers of public authorities with a view to securing a solution of the housing problem and improved systems of communication,

"(*d*) Stimulating interest in and promoting the scientific development of towns so that the evils arising from haphazard growth may in future be avoided;

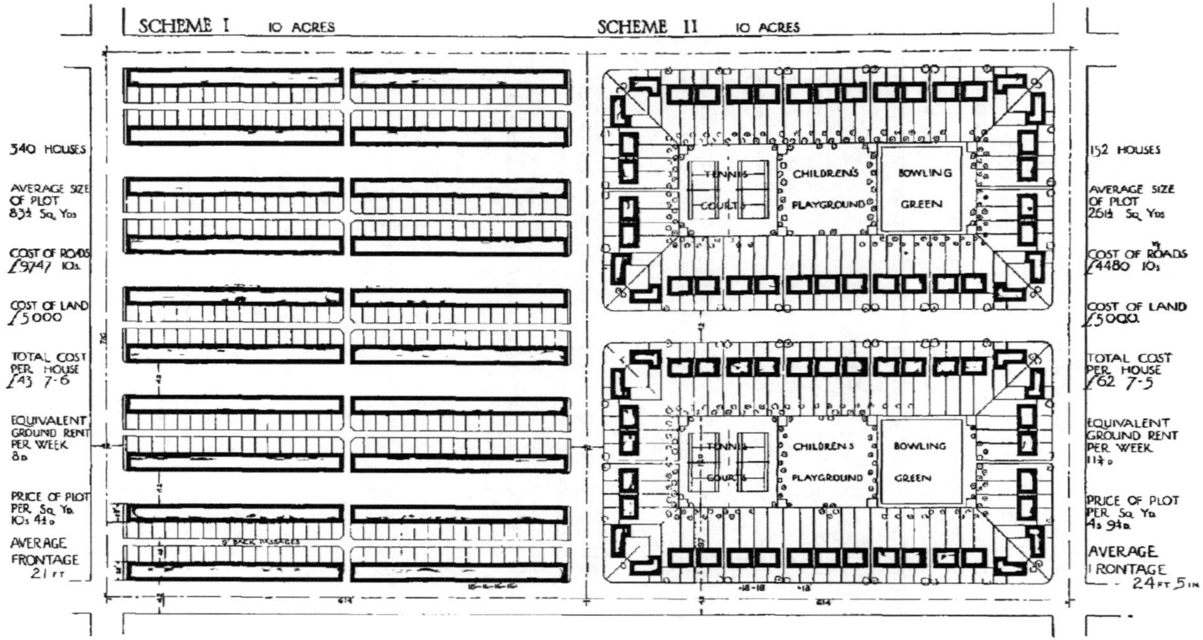

Mr Raymond Unwin's diagram showing the actual financial results of "Garden City" development as compared with the ordinary town development, "(e) Promoting the erection of sanitary and beautiful dwellings with adequate space for gardens and recreation

"Of the above clauses (a) shall be considered the primary work of the Association and the remainder secondary"

The following note was issued with the new rules.—

"It will be seen that this widening of the scope of the Association's work tends greatly to increase its usefulness It is now possible for us not only to advocate the importance and effectiveness of our specific remedy for overcrowding, but to encourage movements of a related character, and to assist other organisations having similar objects in view"

This was, indeed, the first pronouncement of any society or body in England in favour of municipal Town-planning, although that name does not appear yet in the rules

IN 1905.

With the publication of the first official handbook of the Association in 1905 (*The Garden City Movement*, by G Montagu Harris) the rules contained the following objects·—

"To promote the relief of overcrowded areas and to secure a wider distribution of the population over the land

"PRIMARILY, by advocating and assisting in the establishment of Garden Cities (on the principle suggested in Howard's *Garden Cities of To-morrow*) designed from the outset to secure healthful and adequate housing for the whole population, and in which the inhabitants shall become in a collective capacity the owners of the sites, subject to full recognition of public as well as individual interests

"SECONDARILY, by encouraging the tendency of manufacturers to remove their works from congested centres to the country, by co-operating or advising with such firms, public bodies, and other associations to secure better housing accommodation for workpeople near to their places of employment; by taking steps to promote effective legislation with this end in view; and by generally advocating the ordered design and development of towns."

IN 1906.

In 1906 the increasing activities of the Association and the growth of that part relating to the establishment of Garden Suburbs resulted in a further definition of its work, and the Objects then appeared as follows :—

"(I) *The building of new towns in country districts on well-thought-out principles, such as the Garden City at Letchworth*, designed from the outset to secure the healthful and adequate housing of its whole population, so that the land shall never become overcrowded with houses, and the town, when built, shall be permanently surrounded by a wide belt of agricultural and park lands.

"(II) *The creation of Garden Suburbs*, such as the Hampstead Garden Suburb, on similar principles for the immediate relief of existing towns

"(III) *The building of Garden Villages*, as exemplified by Port Sunlight and Bournville, for properly housing the working classes near their work.

"(IV) *The acquisition of open spaces*, and the improvement of existing towns and villages on Garden City principles.

"(V) *The removal of factories* from congested areas to country districts.

"(VI) *The provision of small holdings* in proximity to towns, together with measures for the disposal of agricultural produce to the advantage of the home producer and consumer "

A point of great importance to be noted here is the dropping of definitions such as appeared in earlier rules, an indication of the fact that by now the meaning of the terms had become well enough understood to make it unnecessary to repeat them even in the rules. In view of the shocking misuse of the title term " Garden City " in later days, it will probably be found necessary to formulate some short statement which shall express adequately in what way a true garden city or garden suburb differs from an ordinary building estate or a town planning scheme

The success of Letchworth and the growing necessity for securing legislation enabling towns to control their extensions is shown in further expansion of the Objects, and in the alteration of the title of the Association. The name Garden Cities and Town Planning Association was decided upon by the Council in the year 1907 and in February, 1908, the name of the monthly official organ (started in 1904) was changed from *The Garden City* to *Garden Cities and Town Planning* In that issue it was stated, " In using the plural ' Garden Cities,' instead of ' Garden City,' too, we hope still further to emphasise the fact that we are not concerned solely with Letchworth, but that our work is much wider, and, we hope, of more far-reaching effect even than that scheme Nothwithstanding this, Letchworth has our first claim to notice, as it is in the success of First Garden City Limited that our hope rests for future endeavour upon the same lines."

IN 1909.

In July, 1909, again in order to meet changing circumstances, the Objects were adopted in the following form :—

(*a*) To promote Town Planning.

(*b*) To advise on, draw up schemes for, and establish Garden Cities, Garden Suburbs, and Garden Villages.

(*c*) Housing and the improvement of its sanitation.

(*d*) The collection and publication of information as to the above.

(*e*) The education of public opinion by lantern lectures, cheap literature, conferences, etc.

(*f*) The influencing and promotion of legislation

(*g*) The improvement of local by-laws.

The question of small holdings, although an integral part of Garden City promotion, was dropped from the rules in consequence of an agreement come to between various bodies concerned with small holdings to amalgamate into one central body. At the same time the rules were changed in other respects to allow the Association to take up what has become an important part of its work, namely, the arrangement of educational tours in Great Britain and abroad.

IN 1913.

Perhaps the next development of importance was in January, 1913, when I was despatched as the representative of the Association on a missionary lecture tour throughout the United States and Canada. That tour lasted over three months, in the course of which I travelled about thirty thousand miles and gave seventy-five lectures and addresses in the principal cities. The result of that experiment is an enormous interest in our publications and work from all parts of the Continent, and the establishment of several societies in affiliation with the parent body.

The growth of interest in the over-seas empire prompted the suggestion as far back as 1911 that a lecturer be sent to Australasia, and in 1912 this was definitely decided upon, a special colonial department being organised and arrangements being made, now, happily, almost concluded, for a systematic visit by a competent lecturer

These activities, combined with the interchange of visits with other nationalities led up to the formation of the International Garden Cities and Town Planning Association, for the purpose of linking up existing organisations and of extending still farther the knowledge of garden city principles

October, 1913 EWART G. CULPIN

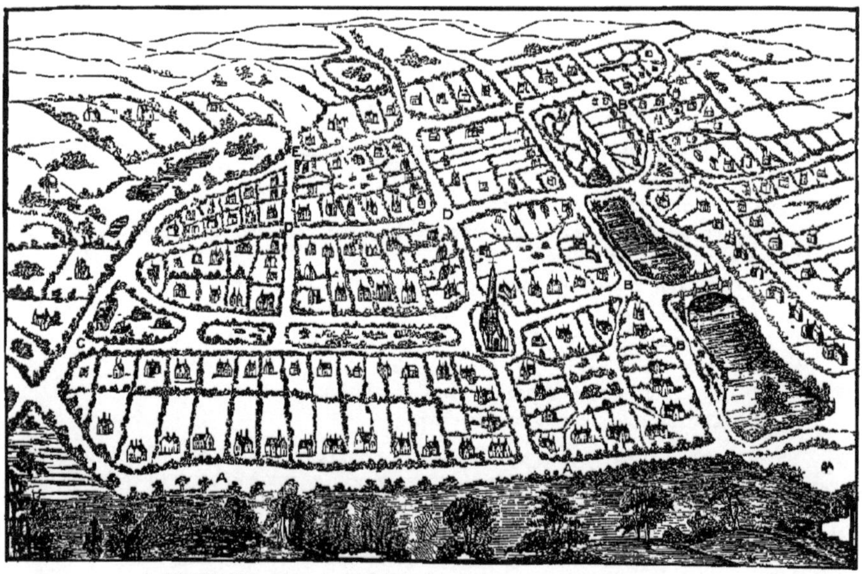

A PROPOSAL FOR A GARDEN VILLAGE AT ILFORD IN 1845

The present suburb occupies part of the site

Meadow Way, Letchworth.

Westholm, Letchworth (Garden City Tenants).

Norton Common, Letchworth, showing cottages in the distance. This beautiful open space of over 70 acres is situated in the centre of the Garden City, only a few minutes' walk from the factory and shopping areas, and adjoining the cottage quarter.

Meadow Way and Lytton Avenue, Letchworth.

PARTICULARS OF ESTATES.

In addition to those estates described in alphabetical order here, the societies connected with Co-partnership Tenants Ltd., Rural Co-partnership, and Co-operative Housing are dealt with under those headings.

LETCHWORTH.

Letchworth, the first and only proper Garden City, rightly comes first under consideration here, both chronologically and because of its size and importance from the historical and economic aspects. The estate, of now 4,566 acres, is the property of First Garden City Ltd., a company with a dividend limited to 5 per cent. cumulative, whose memoranda and articles embody the root principles of the movement The town is situated thirty-four miles from London on the Great Northern Railway, just beyond the old market town of Hitchin. It is served also by the Midland Railway from Hitchin, and being bounded by the Great North Road traffic facilities are excellent.

Letchworth was the first child of the Garden City Movement, and is still the only town where an attempt is being made to put into practice Mr Ebenezer Howard's suggestions in his book "Garden Cities of To-morrow." The Garden Cities Association promoted a "Pioneer Company" for the purpose of finding a suitable site for the new town, and £5,000 was subscribed for investigating the available estates. The very best advice in the country was drawn upon, and as a consequence Letchworth was selected and the "Pioneer Company" obtained options over the land, which was held by fourteen different owners. First Garden City Ltd. was then formed to take over the options and develop the estate. The authorised capital was £300,000, but less than a quarter of this was subscribed at the outset, the whole idea being new, and the limited dividend appealing only to a limited investing public. Confidence in the movement has grown with every stage of progress at Letchworth, and although a dividend has not been declared, net profits are being made, and the capital value of the estate has almost been doubled, so that the financial success of the scheme is abundantly proved.

Despite all, Letchworth is an astounding success. To its example, more than to anything else, is due, without doubt, the present interest in Town Planning and Housing in this country, and it has also resulted in influencing development in practically the whole civilised world.

First Garden City Ltd., being the owners of what was practically virgin land, have had themselves to provide the necessary equipment of the town, which, in the case of the garden suburbs, is derived from neighbouring towns. Thus the company own the gas, water, and electric light undertakings, they have made the roads; they provide and maintain the sewers and the sewage disposal works; and they have organised such facilities as an omnibus service, swimming bath, etc., to encourage the growth and amenities of the town

Besides the by-laws of the Hitchin Rural District Council, under whose jurisdiction

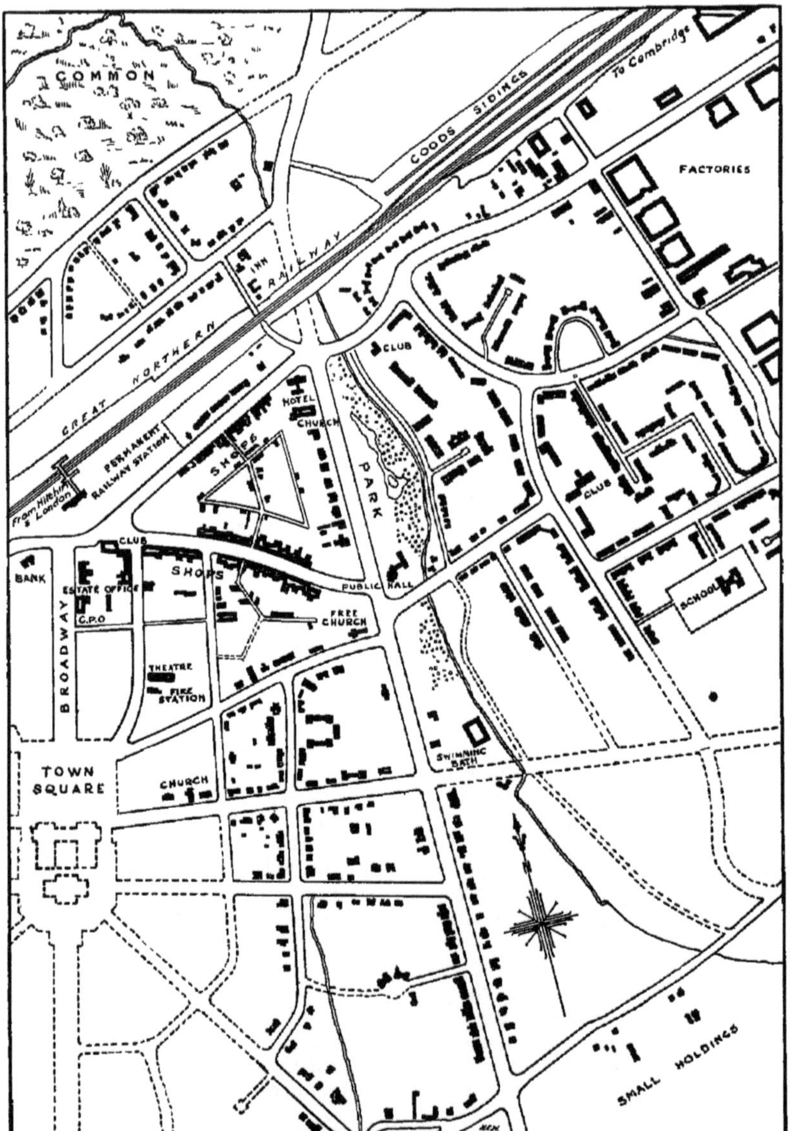

PART OF LETCHWORTH GARDEN CITY,
Showing details of lay-out, workmen's cottages adjoining the factory area, and the central Town Square.

Letchworth is, the company has its own building regulations and its surveyor exercises some supervision over designs and specifications to ensure proper conditions being observed. The maximum of houses allowed to the acre is twelve, but as the size of the house increases so does the area of the plot, so that all over the building area (which is 1,200 acres only, the remainder being agricultural and park land) there will probably be an average of not more than half that number. An ultimate population of 30,000 people is provided for on the town area, or 35,000 including the agricultural belt, dealt with in the introductory article Thus, over the whole of the seven square miles of Garden City, there will be an average of only nine people to the acre, compared with the two or three hundred still allowed by the by-laws of many towns.

The agricultural belt of 3,000 acres marks a fundamental difference between Letchworth and every other experiment on garden city lines and, indeed, distinguishes it from every other town in the world. Many places have belts or girdles of green, but none has a definite provision such as this; and as in the town the way is pointed for a new tradition of development, so it is hoped that the agricultural belt will help in the solution of some of the rural problems. A good deal of attention has been given to small holdings, especially in the direction of milk production, and recently an exhaustive inquiry has been made with a view to assisting in this development.

To secure the proper carrying out of the objects of the company leasehold tenure is in vogue, on easy terms, and for either 99 or 999 years. Freehold is granted only for such purposes as churches, etc, or where land is acquired by local authorities

The estate has been the scene of two cottage exhibitions and has always shown interesting examples of both cottage and other styles of architecture, while cottages recently erected are probably the most satisfactory yet provided in this country. The cheapest rent is 4s 3d., including rates, which stand at 5s, but these were built before the recent serious advance in building costs.

In addition to the county roads already existing the company have made about ten miles of new roads, and provided nearly twenty miles of water main, fifteen miles of gas mains and fourteen miles of sewers The roads vary from 10 feet to 100 feet, at costs varying from 15s. to £5 per yard run, and exhibit every style of treatment known to modern advocates of town planning. Grass margins and trees are usual, and the practice has obtained of planting fruit trees and borders of herbaceous plants, while in the business quarters flowering shrubs have been planted. Five miles of roads have so far been taken over by the Hertfordshire County Council.

The past year was an important one in the history of the estate, as it was the first year in which a *substantial* profit was made The net profit, after paying all expenses and interest on borrowed capital, amounted to £3,086 12s. 2d. This improvement is on the increase, and it may confidently be asserted that the enterprise is within sight of the dividend-paying period During the year 197 inhabited houses and factories and workshops were added, making a total of 1,761 The number is now nearly 1,900. The ground rents created up to September 30th, 1912, amounted to £5,922.

An important side of the Letchworth experiment, and indeed the crucial test, is the development of its factory area. If Mr Howard's theory had not been sound, manufacturers would not have gone to Letchworth and the place would never have developed. There are now some thirty industries established in the town, and several of these have been very considerably extended. The trades represented include engineering, printing, embroidery, bookbinding, photographic utensils, joinery works, pottery, weaving, commercial motor engineers, motor car makers, metal works, organ builders, seed and implement factories,

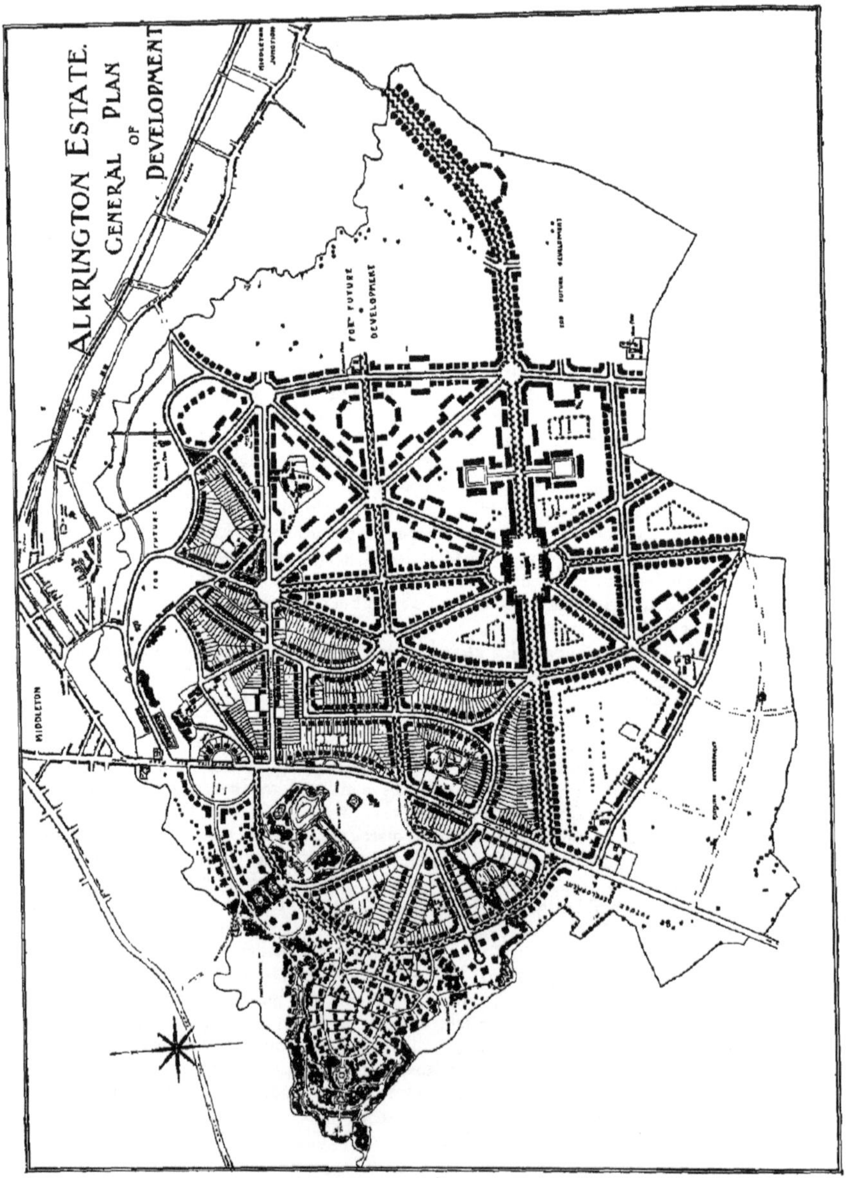
ALKRINGTON ESTATE.
GENERAL PLAN OF DEVELOPMENT
MIDDLETON
FOR FUTURE DEVELOPMENT

scientific instrument makers, colour printers, corset makers, etc. There are five building companies working on the estate. An interesting feature is the co-operative house "Homesgarth"

The town is complete with every facility for commerce, trade and social life. Its residential facilities are excellent, and as a place of residence alone it is being much sought after. The industrial population have here advantages which have been possessed by no other town in the country. Its housing is good, the gardens are ample, and there are many opportunities for recreation and social life. Church life and education are well provided for There are several public halls, and the arrangements for water, lighting and sanitation are as near perfect as they can be. Its scope is infinitely greater and presents the solution of more serious problems than any suburb of a town can possibly do.

Letchworth has been described as England's healthiest town. Both with regard to the general death-rate and infantile mortality the figures are far below any other place in the country.

ALEXANDRIA.

A society, known as the Vale of Leven Tenants Ltd, has been formed at Alexandria for the development on Co-partnership lines of about 6 acres of land within a mile of Loch Lomond. The society is registered under the Industrial and Provident Societies Act, and the capital has been raised by shares and loan stock The land on which the cottages are built has been granted by the Argyll Motor Company—whose workers have formed the Society—free of feu-duty for five years and at the modified rate of £15 per acre thereafter. Good progress is being made. Sixteen houses are now being built.

ALKRINGTON.

It is announced that the Alkrington Hall Estate, Manchester, is to be developed as a Garden Suburb, and it is expected that a large portion of the development will be on Co-partnership lines. The Estate, which consists of about 700 acres and adjoins the Borough of Middleton, possesses many attractive features. Some three or four years ago a strong attempt was made by the Garden City Association to form a Company to acquire this land for Garden City purposes. The Prospecting and Development Committee had surveys made, and local meetings were held, but there was not sufficient response to justify the formation of a Company Although unsuccessful in that respect, the Association had the pleasure of knowing that the Estate was to be laid out on proper lines, and Mr Thomas Adams, who as Hon. Secretary of the Association, had taken much interest in the project, was called in by the owners, the Lees Trustees, as expert adviser. The Estate is now being developed by Messrs. Pepler and Allen on the basis of twelve houses to the acre, with ample provision for recreation grounds and other open space. Good progress has been made already. The first house was opened by Mr. T. C. Horsfall on July 29th, 1911, and building has since progressed steadily. This scheme was one of the first to be submitted to a local authority as a Town Planning Scheme under the Act, and it is interesting to know that Messrs. Pepler and Allen have been able to come to a mutually satisfactory give-and-take arrangement with the Middleton Corporation.

A Co-partnership Housing Society known as "The Alkrington Housing Society Ltd.," has recently undertaken the erection of thirty houses.

ALTON PARK.

An attempt at the proper Town Planning of a seaside resort, a much neglected art, has been begun at Clacton-on-Sea, and the Alton Park Estate of about 100 acres has been laid out on ample Town Planning lines The Estate will be purely residential, and the houses will be mostly of the seaside bungalow type, on plots averaging 40 feet wide by 150 feet deep, and numbering about eight to the acre. Several of the roads are 50 feet wide with 24 feet carriage way, two 6 feet paths, and two 7 feet grass margins planted with trees. Sundry spaces and greens are provided, and the general arrangement is intended to produce good facilities of communication, pleasant aspects and vistas, and satisfactory terminal features. The Estate adjoins the Golf Links The design for the development has been prepared by Messrs. Pepler and Allen.

BLACKLEY.

The Blackley estate of the Manchester Corporation was started in 1901, before the limitations now generally imposed in Garden Cities and Suburbs came in for wide acceptance. It covers a total area of 243 acres, about 2½ miles from Crumpsall (L. and Y), and situated about four miles from Manchester itself It is owned and controlled by the Manchester Corporation About nine acres have been developed with 150 houses thereon. In addition some thirteen acres have been set aside for open spaces, and fifty for small holdings and allotments Excluding the open spaces, the density allowed is seventeen houses per acre. Ultimately the estate is designed to carry 2,810 houses, with a total population of about 11,240. At the present time there are 600 people resident there The minimum size of plots allowed is 300 square yards The death-rate is: general, 13.70, infantile, 102 The cheapest house costs £223, and lets at 6s. 4d. per week including rates, which total 8s 1d. in the £. The maximum rent is 7s (rates included)

The main roads are laid out sixty feet wide and tree-planted, whilst the minor roads are not less than forty-two feet in width.

BOURNVILLE.

Mr Ebenezer Howard has often remarked that it was the inspiration of Bournville which largely affected his vision of the Garden City. Situated close outside Birmingham, the village was originated by Mr George Cadbury as an experiment in the solving of the housing question The main part of the village dates from the year 1895 It is not primarily for the employees of Messrs Cadbury Bros, and there is no private gain, the whole of the estate having been vested in the Bournville Village Trust The revenue is to be spent on the estate, and when this is developed is to be employed elsewhere in building manufacturing villages where not more than one-fifteenth of the total area shall be occupied by factories and one-tenth shall be open spaces. It may also be employed in furthering the interests of good housing generally, and in pursuance of this the funds for the Town Planning Lectureship, recently established at Birmingham University, are supplied by the Trust.

An important recent addition to the public buildings has been made, in the erection of a new Infants' School, which has been presented to the estate by Mr. and Mrs George Cadbury. The following statistics for Bournville may be of interest —Total area, 609 acres; density, 25 persons per acre; population, 4,390. Death-rate, 4 9; infant mortality, 49 6. Land developed 153 acres, open spaces 18 acres. Total houses 925 (inclusive of 38 the property of the Almshouse Trust); houses per acre 6. Cheapest house cost £171, maximum rent, 11s. 6d (rates extra) The cheapest cottage, containing two bedrooms, living-room and scullery, with garden attached, is let at 4/9 per week (rates not included) Cost of development about £250 per acre

The Trustees are arranging for the development of a further portion of their land by means of a Public Utility Society

BOURNVILLE TENANTS LIMITED.

The Bournville Village Trust in 1906 leased twenty acres of its holding to the Co-partnership Society known as Bournville Tenants Limited The maximum dividend is limited to 5 per cent., the last paid being 4 per cent. For every nine acres of land which the Society takes from the Trust one acre is allowed for open spaces, and for every £3,000 subscribed by the Society the Trust advances a loan of £1,000, until the total by this means has reached £28,000. The amount of share capital issued to date is £9,690, and the loan stock £22,043. At present 142 houses are built at a maximum density of eleven per acre The minimum rent (rates and taxes excluded) is 6s per week Tree-planted roads, 42 feet wide, are general to the estate, and cost £4 5s. per yard run. The total area is twenty acres, and only four more houses have to be built to reach the ultimate number expected, viz, 146, which will provide for a population of 750.

BRISTOL GARDEN SUBURB.

Bristol Garden Suburb Ltd. was formed in 1909 to acquire and develop an estate at Shirehampton on Garden City lines, on the principles advocated by the Garden City Association, and the dividend is limited to 5 per cent. The present area of 26 acres can be extended very considerably should the scheme prove attractive The share capital is ten thousand £1 shares. A number of attractive houses have already been built by the Company. In 1910 twenty-three houses were erected and the roads required for the first area of $7\frac{1}{2}$ acres were completed, since which date twenty-one houses have been added, making forty-four in all It is expected that the ultimate number of houses on the present area will be 280, the maximum allowed being fourteen to the acre

It is hoped to form a Co-partnership Society, the initial expenses of which have already been guaranteed by a member of the Board, to undertake further building operations

CAERPHILLY CO-OPERATIVE GARDEN VILLAGE.

The Caerphilly Co-operative Garden Village Society, which is the most advanced in South Wales, owns ten acres of land on the main road between Caerphilly and Llanbradach Eight semi-detached houses have been erected and are letting at 5s 6d a week exclusive of rates, and a further sixteen are being proceeded with as the next instalment of 100 houses. The land is situated at a point of great strategic importance in respect of the future developments of this district, the population of which will almost certainly double or treble during the next ten years through the development of the existing collieries, and the sinking of three other pits which are now projected. Alderman J. E. Evans (president), and Mr. Joseph Howells (chairman), both members of the Glamorgan County Council, and Mr Hubert Jenkins, Miners' agent and member of the Caerphilly Council, were amongst the founders of the Society.

CARDIFF WORKERS' GARDEN VILLAGE SOCIETY.

The Cardiff Workers Garden Village Society has been established for the purpose of building the first real garden suburb in Wales for both middle-class and working-class inhabitants. Eighteen acres of land have been purchased situated close to Rhubina Halt on the new Cardiff Railway. The architectural scheme has been most carefully considered by Mr. A. H. Mottram, Architect of the Housing Reform Company Limited, who are Managers for the Society A striking plan for the site, including altogether 110 acres over which the Society has an option, was prepared by Mr. Raymond Unwin The vistas, closes, and other features are similar to the best characters of the Hampstead Garden Suburb, but there is rather more spaciousness, and a feature is being made of enclosed children's playgrounds at the backs of gardens in each block of houses. The charm of the beautiful wooded hills bordering the site is a great asset. The character of the architecture is rough-cast and stone with grey or green slate roofs, red brick and tiles being excluded altogether from the estate as not suitable to the character of the country, which lies in a district where stone is the natural material.

The fact that this Society's land is reached in ten minutes by train from the centre of Cardiff, is making it popular, and the applications for houses considerably exceed in number the thirty-four houses now being erected. The Society is building by direct labour under the management of Mr. J. O. West, late manager for the Hampstead Tenants.

CARLISLE.

A Co-partnership Society, called Newby West Tenants Limited, has been formed for developing 20 acres to the west of the City There is a great demand for cottages locally and the undertaking starts with every prospect of support.

CAXTON GARDENS COTTAGE CLUB.

The Caxton Gardens Cottage Club, founded in 1906, is a small industrial concern promoted by Messrs. Billing & Sons Ltd., Printers, Guildford It is solely a co-operative venture, which has erected twenty-four houses for the employees alone at a cost of £5,688, the land costing £1,250 in addition The occupants pay 8s 2d per week for house and garden, with rates extra In twenty years they will have repaid capital outlay and interest on the scheme, and the houses become their own property. The houses are well built in pairs on allotments restricted to 21¼ feet frontage and 120 feet depth. In front, separated by a 9 feet gravelled pathway, is a large triangular piece of ground laid out as a lawn, with a shrubbery on the side nearest the road. Each occupier owns a twenty-fourth part. There is little in the scheme which illustrates or has reference to the principles of Garden Cities and Suburbs, but it has proved a successful venture in co-operation, and represents a notable improvement in ordinary housing conditions.

CLYDEBANK GARDEN SUBURB.

The difficulty of raising capital is preventing very rapid advance with the Clydebank Co-partnership Society, which was initiated three years ago The first few houses, are, however, being proceeded with, and it is hoped that as knowledge of the movement and of co-partnership principles makes headway among the local manufacturers there may be more response to the appeal for capital for the housing of their workpeople.

COVENTRY.

Coventry Garden Suburb is one of the most interesting of the recent schemes with which the Garden Cities and Town Planning Association have been connected. Through the public-spirited interest of Mr. T A. Cash a start is being made on fourteen acres of land in the only unspoiled district of this beautiful old city, which is desecrated by acres of 12-feet fronted houses. Coventry Garden Suburbs Ltd is to be conducted on Co-partnership lines, with a 5 per cent. dividend. An option over the adjoining land, which belongs to charity trustees, is being secured, and development promises to be rapid The first roads taken in hand have been completed and all the houses occupied. The Society suffers from the oppression of the local by-laws, and representation has been made to the Local Government Board and the local Council with the idea of obtaining modifications of the clauses relating to widths of roads and heights of rooms. Nowhere in the country is an example of good lay-out more wanted, and it is hoped that the facilities asked for will be granted.

The land is held on lease for ninety-nine years, renewable for further similar terms at option, at a low progressive rent, which will not exceed £22 an acre. These terms are exceptionally favourable and may be commended to owners desirous of advancing housing

CUFFLEY GARDEN VILLAGE.

This scheme is another tribute to the work of the Garden Cities and Town Planning Association, the Secretary having induced the owner to arrange the development of his land on Garden City lines The estate consists of nearly 550 acres, in a most beautiful part of Hertfordshire, and including scenery probably superior to that of any other "garden city" scheme in existence Cuffley is the last station on the Great Northern Railway Enfield to Stevenage loop line, as at present constructed The estate is beautifully wooded, and rises to an altitude of over 350 feet. A preliminary plan has been prepared by Messrs. Pepler & Allen. Development is now proceeding and gas, water and main drainage have all been provided, some large houses are being built, and a Tenants Society has commenced operations. A golf links occupying 123 acres has been laid out, so that quite a quarter of the whole estate will be kept as open space.

DARLINGTON GROVE GARDEN SUBURB.

Although differing in its inception from other schemes, this is of interest as being a practical attempt by working builders, on ordinary commercial lines, to provide houses designed and planned on Garden City principles—with a limited number of houses to the acre. The cottages, of which twenty-six are completed, are situated near Thorne, in the South Yorkshire coalfield They occupy a splendid site, fronting the main highway from Sheffield to Hull, and are intended for the employees of the Moor End Colliery of Messrs. Pease & Partners Limited The weekly rents have been fixed at 6s., including rates. Mr A W Shelton, F.C.I., Estate Agent, of Nottingham, who is well known as an active member of the Advisory Committee of the National Housing and Town Planning Council, is responsible for having prevailed on the builders, Messrs. J Tilley & Co., of Nottingham, to depart from their original intention of building about forty houses to the acre—a system which has most lamentably been followed in most of the newly erected colliery districts near Doncaster. The scheme is intended to give about 120 houses on 8½ acres of land.

DIDSBURY GARDEN SUBURB.

This small scheme, which is being carried out by the Didsbury Garden Suburb Provident Co-operative Society Limited, owes its origin to the local members of the Garden City Association. It is situated five miles from Manchester, and the local station adjoins the estate. During 1909 an additional plot of land was purchased. The area of this suburb is just over two acres, and the number of houses allowed per acre is fifteen. Twenty houses have been completed and tenanted, and there are applications for others as soon as they are completed The plot of ground used as a playground has been secured upon a trust deed for ever. The promoters believe that societies such as this should be possible in every village, if the question of capital is solved Homes cost from £230 to £250, and rentals are from 7s. 9d to 9s rates included. Each tenant is a share-holder, and receives 5 per cent. on his investment

The Second Didsbury Garden Suburb Ltd. (1911), comprises fourteen houses, with large gardens, at rentals varying from 7s 9d. to 9s per week. The tenants are the share-holders, and five of them form the management committee The sum of £120 has already been cleared off the mortgagee's account, after paying the sum of £44 18s. od to tenant shareholders as bonus on rent, at two shillings in the pound, a very satisfactory result for a new society.

FAIRFIELD TENANTS.

This Society owns twenty-two acres situated half way between Manchester and Ashton, in a district containing large industries, where there is a great demand for houses. There are good gardens provided and reservations are made for recreational purposes The streets are tree-planted, with grass margins. The majority of the houses will be for working men. Baths, hot and cold water, and electric light are included in all houses, which will be let at from 5s to 10s a week

FALLINGS PARK.

Fallings Park is an estate of 400 acres, situate about one mile and a half from the London and North-Western Railway station at Wolverhampton, on the property of Sir Richard Paget, Bart. The site is in touch with the city by tramway and motor bus Development began in 1907, when the Fallings Park Garden Suburb Tenants came into existence. The Society has now about eight acres under its control, and some 75 houses built It is intended to extend this type of development indefinitely, so that the greater part of the 400 acres may be held by one or more co-partnership tenant societies Large works on a site of ten acres adjoining the estate have been erected by Messrs Chubb and Sons, and other factories are arriving on the estate

The original scheme was under the control of Mr Thos. Adams. The advent of a new railway has necessitated an entirely fresh scheme which is being prepared by Prof Adshead and Messrs Pepler & Allen, who will have charge of future development

FALLSIDE.

Messrs Brown & Polson have started a small scheme for the accommodation of the employees in their Paisley works Six blocks of four houses each have been erected on a site about a mile from the town, and another six blocks are now being built. Forty-eight families are being provided for. Previously these were living under the prevailing Scottish conditions of "a room and a kitchen," and the new homes provide two rooms, with kitchen, scullery, etc , so that the sexes may be decently provided for. The houses are well designed and have tasteful elevations. The rent charged is £12 and £12 10s a year, including rates, but this is not an economic return, producing about 2½ per cent only on the outlay

FFORESTFACH.

One of the first attempts at a Garden Suburb in South Wales was that at Fforestfach, a small mining village near Swansea. The first scheme of eight acres was initiated by Messrs Pepler and Allen early in 1910 Many difficulties were met with, but there is now every sign of good progress. The cottages are being built with 18 in. local stone walls,

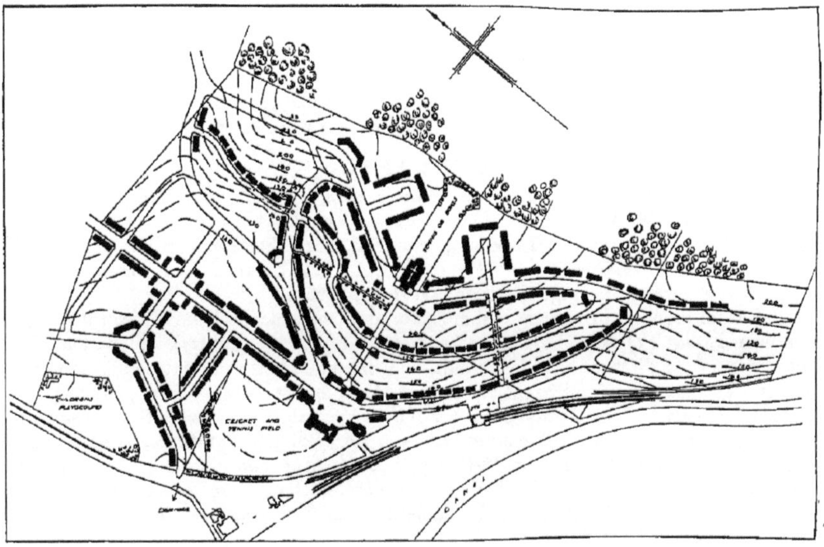

PLAN OF GLASGOW GARDEN SUBURB.

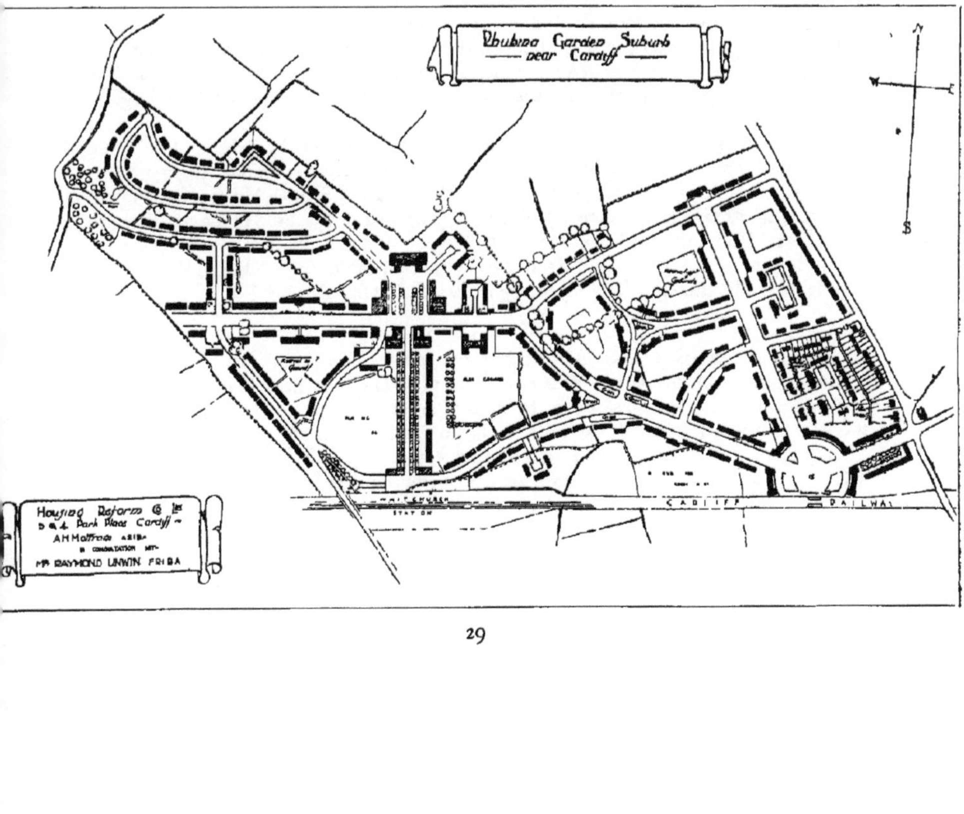

and are therefore extremely solid and fit in well with the old tradition of the place. One hundred houses are provided for, and there is a curved 60 ft main tree-planted avenue down to the centre designed for continuation when the adjoining lands are developed. Space has been left for allotments, bowling-green, and playground.

A Co-partnership Housing Society has recently commenced operations.

GIDEA PARK.

The Gidea Park Estate, "Romford Garden Suburb," first came into prominence in May, 1910, when development on modified garden city lines was begun It is openly a commercial venture, with no limitation of dividend, but it has been embarked upon with wide application of good principles. The present plan was the result of a competition held in conjunction with the Cottage Exhibition at the Suburb

The total area of the estate is about 500 acres, of which 108 have been developed. London is distant 13½ miles by rail, the nearest station being Squirrels Heath and Gidea Park. Already 188 houses have been built, and the estate has a present population of 700 persons. The houses are built eight to ten to the acre, and rents range from £100 to £30 per annum (rates extra) The ultimate number of houses expected is 4,000, with provision for a population of 16,000 Some five acres has been set aside and developed as open spaces, and, in addition, the estate has an 18-hole golf course over ninety acres. Small holdings or allotments are not yet provided for. The average width of the roads is forty feet, and all have turf margins and are tree planted. Some three miles of roads are now completed with water, sewerage, and gas mains.

GLASGOW GARDEN SUBURB TENANTS.

The Glasgow Garden Suburb Tenants Ltd has now passed the initial stages, and contracts have been placed for sixty houses, of which over forty are nearing completion. The demand for the houses has been most encouraging. An option has been secured over several hundred acres comprising undulating land, with hedgerows and woods, and commanding extensive views of the country on the outskirts of Glasgow at Garscube The estate adjoins an extensive golf course, and is abundantly sheltered by trees. The proposal to lay out this Suburb on the most approved lines urgently requires realisation in order that the concrete example can be brought to the doors of the great Scotish Metropolis, and act as an incentive to other similar schemes, which are proposed in the Vale of Leven, Greenock, Renfrew, etc The capital of the Society is £50,000 and the Committee of management includes Sir John Stirling Maxwell, Bart., Sir Samuel Chisholm, Bart., Bailie W F Russell, Ex-Bailie Wm. Martin, etc. The Secretary is Mr. M Boyd Auld

GLYN CORY.

The garden village of Glyn Cory is situated seven miles from Cardiff and is close to Peterston Station on the Great Western Railway The site rises from 90 to 350 feet above sea level, with a gentle slope in the form of an amphitheatre. The area of the estate is 300 acres, of which 160 will be built on, 80 for golf course, and 60 for allotments and small holdings. Provision is made for 1,400 houses, with an ultimate population of 5,000 and 6,000. The estate is private property, and the land is let out on leases of 99 and 999 years The rent is charged from ¾d to 2d per yard, or about one-fourth the rental of similar land in Cardiff A scheme is also in operation whereby residents can obtain 75 per cent. of the money required for building purposes at 4 per cent. interest, repayable in ten to twenty years Mr John Cory initiated the enterprise, and since his death it has been looked after by Mr Reginald Cory

GOUROCK AND GREENOCK TENANTS.

This, the first co-partnership Society registered in Scotland, has opened its first blocks of houses. As is the case elsewhere in Scotland, loan stock is difficult to secure, and this is illustrated by the fact that the amount of share capital is three times as large as that of the loan stock The shareholders are principally artisans in the Royal Naval Torpedo factory, who since their transfer from Woolwich have had great difficulty in obtaining suitable housing, the tenement system of the district not meeting with the southern ideas. It is proposed to build 500 houses

HAMPDEN PARK ESTATE.

Hampden Park Estate, on the outskirts of Eastbourne, is not a garden city, nor a co-partnership suburb, in their true sense It is due to a venture dating back to 1888, which is now the Eastbourne Artisans and Labourers' Improved Dwellings Company Limited. The housing settlement, known as Hampden Park Estate, was opened in 1909, when 60 houses, nine to twelve to the acre, were taken up. The houses face 50 feet tree-planted roads, and are set back with 100 feet between the building lines The rents vary from 8s. 6d to 12s 6d per week, including rates and taxes. The success of the venture decided the Directors to acquire another four acres in 1910, making nine in all. Some 73 houses have now been built on the Company's land, the ultimate provision being 98 houses on nine acres. The Company has paid a dividend of 5 per cent. on capital for some years past.

HAMPSTEAD GARDEN SUBURB.

The second of the great schemes inaugurated on Garden City lines owes it origin to the work of Mrs. S. A. Barnett, the wife of the late Canon Barnett, who, after a lifetime spent in the closest touch with the physical and spiritual needs of the people in the East End of London, saw in Mr Howard's scheme an opening for the improvement of the deadly, soul-killing monotony and hideousness of the average London suburb. Coupled with the scheme was the idea to save a portion of land to be added to Hampstead Heath as an open space for ever, and this was successfully accomplished.

The estate, which is owned by the Hampstead Garden Suburb Trust Ltd , was laid out by Mr. Raymond Unwin, already famous for his work at Letchworth, and in the last three years it has become the best example in the world of modern town planning. Artists and architects from every country under the sun have been to see the work which an unfettered control has been able to effect on the heights of Golder's Green The growth of the Estate has been phenomenal Since the first sod was cut on May 2nd, 1907, 1,550 houses have been built and occupied, with an estimated population of 5,000 people.

The value of the houses and public buildings on the Estate is estimated at £800,000, representing, with the land and roads, a capital value of over £1,000,000, while the ground rent secured amounts to no less than £11,330 out of a total estimated rental of £15,000. Dividends at the rate of 5 per cent. per annum on the ordinary shares have been paid during the past four years.

The end of the first portion of the Estate (240 acres) being in sight, the Directors have acquired another 112 acres of land from the Ecclesiastical Commissioners, while the Co-partnership Tenants Limited, who have been responsible for the development of a large portion of the original area, have taken up 80 acres of the added portion and have also taken 300 acres direct from the same authorities, making a total of one square mile of land, the whole of which will be planned by the Hampstead Garden Suburb Trust Ltd

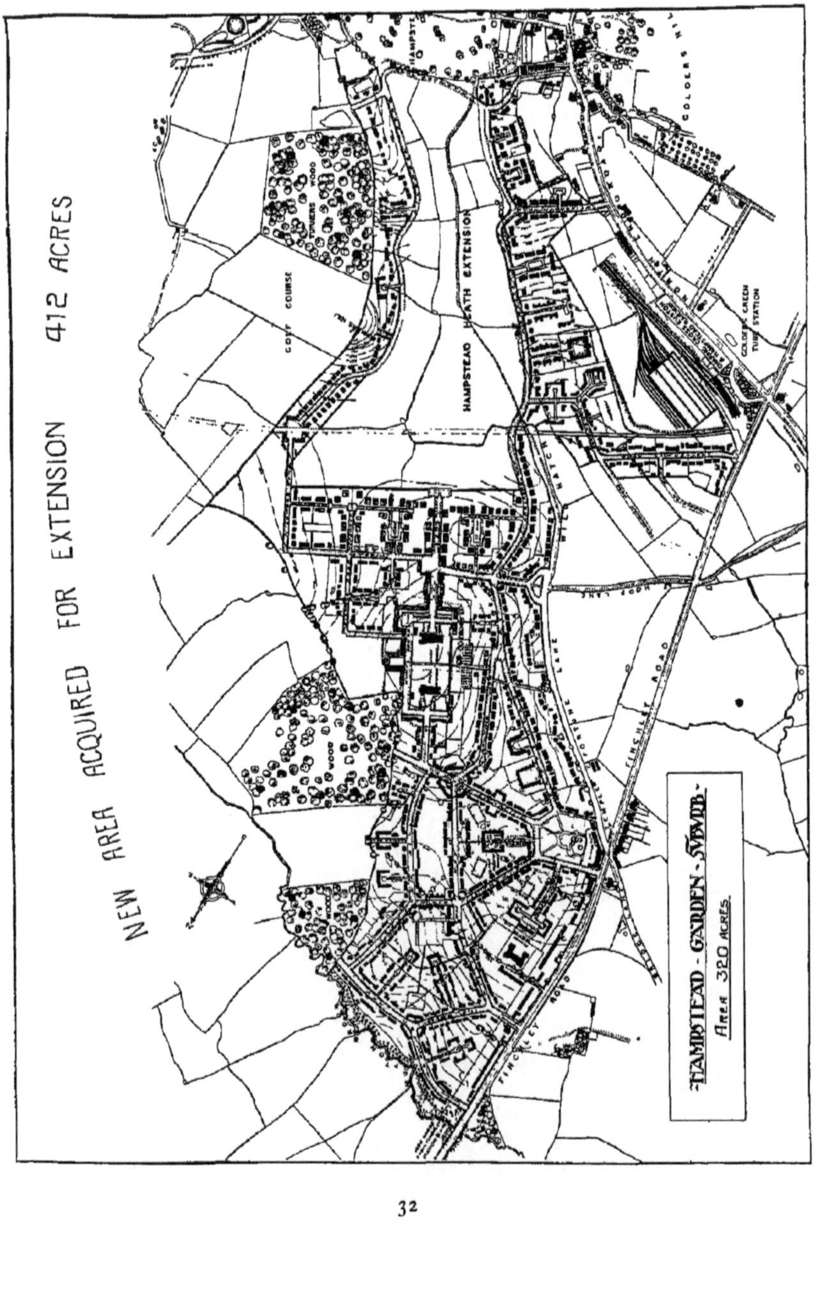
NEW AREA ACQUIRED FOR EXTENSION 412 ACRES
HAMPSTEAD HEATH EXTENSION
GOLF COURSE
GOLDERS GREEN TUBE STATION
FINCHLEY ROAD
HAMPSTEAD - GARDEN - SUBURB -
AREA 320 ACRES

Building operations in the Suburb have been carried out by a variety of enterprise. The Trust has confined itself to erecting housing for its workers, the Institute, and a home for poor children. The Co-partnership Societies have built the larger number of houses, cottages, etc , renting from 5s 9d per week to £110 per year , also the Club House at Willifield Green, and homes for elderly people. The Improved Industrial Dwellings Company have built a number of cottages and houses let at weekly rents from 7s. 6d. to 14s 6d Other companies and builders have built and are building houses to sell from £425 to £3,500.

The following figures of the Garden Suburb are available :—Share capital authorised £75,000, issued £54,000. Authorised debentures £150,000, issued £131,000. Total rates, 5s. 6d. in the £. Houses limited twelve to the acre, with an average of 8 over the whole Estate Maximum rent £110 per year, minimum 6s 6d (rates not included). Average cost of cheapest house £300 Roads made 7 miles Principal roads 40 feet, and others less. Roads are tree-planted and grass margins laid.

HASLEMERE TENANTS LIMITED.

Haslemere Tenants Limited owes its existence to the energies of Mr Aneurin Williams, so well known in connection with Garden City work generally, and particularly as Chairman of First Garden City Limited. A start has been made with an area of about six acres, which is being dealt with carefully, in order to preserve open spaces and to provide economical houses. Land in the neighbourhood of Haslemere is very expensive, and building is very dear, but the success attending the first endeavours of the Company in putting up twenty houses on the first developed parts leads to the hope that other extensions will follow. The ultimate number of houses expected is sixty, and the density per acre will be ten, with a population of approximately 200 The dividend is limited to 5 per cent The main sewer is available for drainage, and the Haslemere Urban District Council supply water from their works at Blackdown. Gas and electric current are available

HEREFORD CO-OPERATIVE HOUSING LIMITED.

Hereford possesses a great distinction over most Garden Village schemes, in that it is the first community of its kind in England to be called into being through the assistance of a municipality In 1909, as the result of consistent effort on the part of several disinterested citizens, an agreement was entered into between the corporation and the above co-operative body for the creation of a Garden Village on a block of eight acres thirty poles, in the city of Hereford The City secured the land and leased it for a period of eighty years to the Company The maximum rent payable till 1932 is not to exceed £133, and after that date for the remainder of the term £62 per annum The actual rent is taken at the cost per year to the City by way of principal, interest and expenses in connection with the loan raised for the purchase and laying out of the land. The terms are such as to ensure the Corporation recovering the whole of the expenditure involved upon the municipality. The cost of the land is repayable in eighty years, but the cost of laying out has to be refunded in twenty-two years An advantage to the Company was that the Corporation secured the money for the purchase of the land at the Government rate of interest. At the end of the term, when all repayments have been made, it is further provided that the Corporation shall hand over the land, other than roads, etc., to the Company without further charge.

Under the agreement the Company pays taxes, and had to provide not less than thirty nor more than 100 separate self-contained houses in two years from the date of signing, and this has been done. Safeguards are provided ensuring that none of the land shall, during the eighty years of lease, be used for advertisement hoardings, music halls, or theatres, noxious trades or a publichouse.

The land cost £1,500 The rents of the houses range from 4s. 9d. to 7s 9d (including rates). The roads are laid out in picturesque curves, and there is a total width of 70 feet between the houses.

The estate has now been completed and eighty-six houses have been erected.

HULL GARDEN VILLAGE.

Situated a mile and a half from Hull Paragon Station, this picturesque Garden Village is an example of a Village within a City It was begun in 1907. The estate, for which Sir James Reckitt, Bart, is mainly responsible, is right in the centre of the town. It covers an area of ninety-four acres, of which seventy have been developed, at a density of twelve houses per acre. Some 560 houses have been built, and it is anticipated that eventually from 640 to 700 homes will be provided The cheapest house costs £180, and is let at 4s. 9d. per week, including rates The maximum rent is £35 and rates The land tenure is freehold, but the houses are let only, all the building being undertaken by the proprietors. The present population is about 2,000 The village is controlled by a private company, with a dividend limited to 3 per cent. Special by-laws enable economies to be made in regard to road construction, but the grass lined thoroughfare characteristic of most of the schemes has not yet been found possible. The widths of road in use are thirty feet, forty feet, and fifty feet, and all are planted with trees

ILFORD GARDEN SUBURB.

This is a direct result of the work of the Garden City and Town Planning Association, and possesses features of exceptional interest, inasmuch as the acquisition of the land was the result of a desire to preserve from the ravages of the ordinary builder, which are only too painfully evident in this suburb, a charming piece of park land, contiguous with the existing park, which was coming into the market No profit is being taken by the promoting Company (Town Planning and Garden Cities Company Ltd), and the whole profits beyond the payment of fees and expenses are to be devoted to public objects in the district. The area of the land is forty acres, and the number of houses will be about seven to the acre. An area of twenty acres of park land, together with the mansion house, stables, conservatories and gardens, was reserved for the extension of the Valentines Park belonging to the Ilford Urban District Council The Company were enabled to offer the proposed extension to the Council at £528 per acre, which the Council accepted, and have recently completed the purchase of the proposed extension, which now forms one of the most attractive features of the Valentines Park. The price of £528 per acre compares very favourably with the £800 per acre paid by the Council for the adjoining fields.

This is one of the many examples of the good work being done by the Association.

JESMOND PARK.

Jesmond Park Estate is situated near Rochdale. It is the property of Mr. S. Smethurst, J.P, President of the National Federation of Building Trade Employers An area of 50 acres is available, of which it is intended to develop 30 acres on the following lines: Houses to average 16 to the acre, roads at least 40 feet wide, with grass margins and trees. The houses are to be built mainly in pairs, with an occasional group of three or four, the minimum cost per house being £200, and it is intended that tenants shall buy their own houses at a weekly charge of 5s. 6d for the cheapest The scheme was hung up

Hull Garden Village.

Wordsworth Walk, Hampstead Garden Suburb.

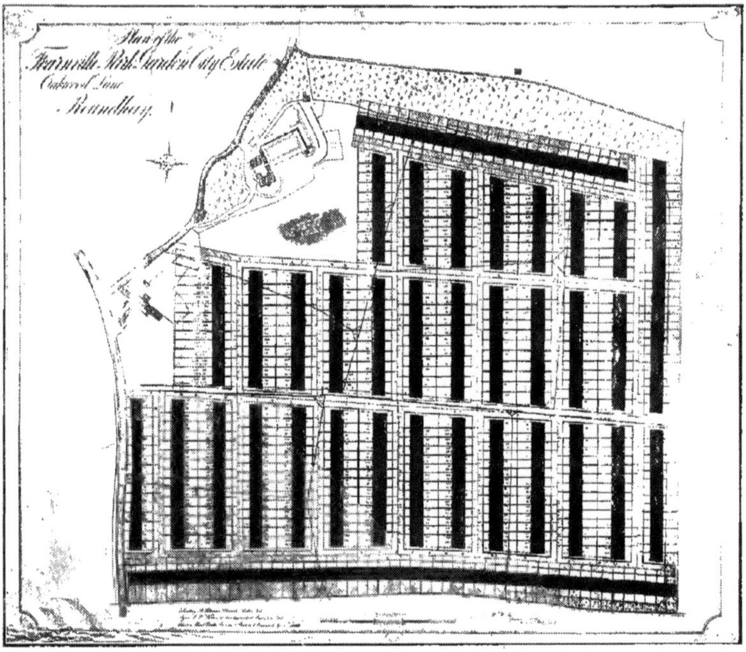

A so-called "Garden City" whose promoters have gone so far as to use the words "Garden City Association" in connection with it. A glance will show the ruthless way in which the plan has been made in entire disregard of all Garden City principles, the rigid straight line having been preserved at the expense of many natural beauties.

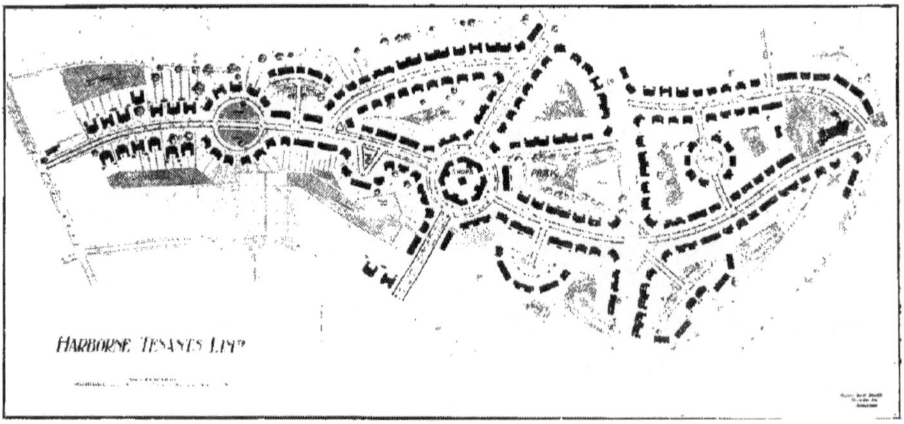

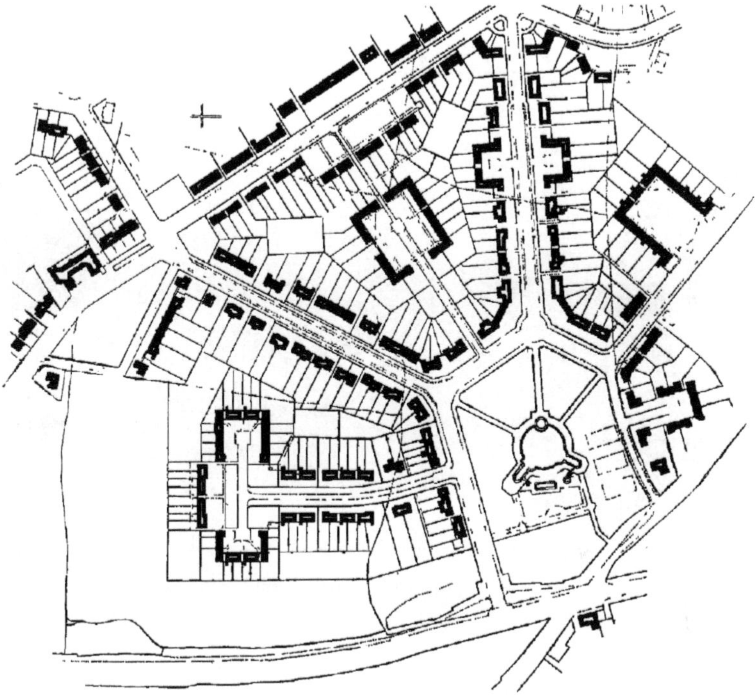

A PLAN OF PART OF THE CO-PARTNERSHIP ESTATE AT HAMPSTEAD
(Showing the care taken in the lay out of the land, and the grouping of the houses under Garden City principles)

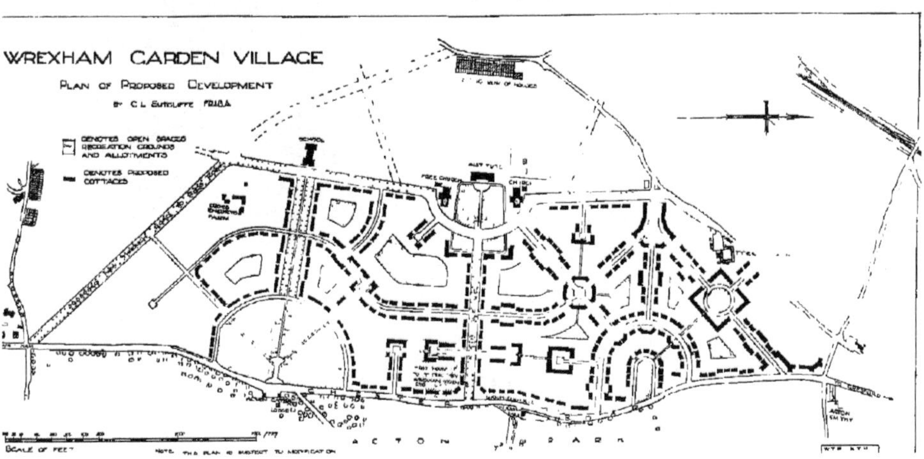

Corner treatment at Hampstead.

owing to the proposals in regard to roads coming into conflict with the Town Council's by-laws, and the subject, according to latest information, is now before the Local Government Board.

KNEBWORTH GARDEN VILLAGE.

This scheme owes its origin to the interest of the Earl of Lytton in Garden City work A considerable part of his estate adjoining the railway station has already been planned and work is progressing. The first beginnings of the village were on the old lines, but now that Lord Lytton, who owns all the land, has had a proper scheme prepared, a happy future is assured, and is being helped greatly by the operations of a development company, Garden Villages Ltd A Co-partnership Society has also been formed and its first houses are all taken by tenant members and new houses are bespoken before erection. The area of this garden village is about 800 acres, with about eight houses to the acre. The total number of houses to be built will thus work out at about 6,400, of which 250 are already erected.

Knebworth is on the Great Northern Railway, thirty-five minutes' run from King's Cross, the estate itself being pierced by the line, down to which the country slopes on either side. The ceremony of cutting the first sod for the Tenant Society was performed on April 20th, 1912, by Mrs Cecil Harmsworth, the speakers being Lord Robert Cecil, Sir Sydney Lea, and Mr. Cecil Harmsworth, M P.

LLANIDLOES.

An estate of nine acres near the little Montgomeryshire Borough of Llanidloes has been acquired privately and will be made over to the Welsh Town Planning and Housing Trust. The Town Recreation Ground is included in the area, and it is intended to build some forty houses as a small adjunct to the town, adjoining the Recreation Ground A co-operative housing society has been formed to do the building, and it is expected that a start will be made in the summer of 1913 The plans have been prepared by Mr. Alwyn Lloyd.

LIVERPOOL'S MUNICIPAL HOUSING.

In 1864 Liverpool possessed the worst slums in England—places that were the haunts of typhoid fever, immorality, crime, and drunkenness Rows of houses four and six storeys high, built back to back, only nine feet apart, were inhabited by about one-fifth of the entire population of the city

The social results of this state of overcrowding were little short of appalling. The death rate averaged sixty per thousand, whilst the homes of the people were never free from infectious disease

Since that time Liverpool has spent considerably over a million sterling, tearing down these filthy slums and re-housing the people who were displaced in model tenements and cottages. The rents for the new houses are let at a figure within the means of the tenants. The poverty of the tenants generally can be imagined when it is stated that several thousands of them subsist on an average of less than 10s. per week, and the greater number on less than 15s. per week More than half of them are casual labourers employed at the docks.

The result of re-housing in Liverpool is an extremely satisfactory indication that large cities faced with large slum problems should take a bold and vigorous policy. Liverpool's figures up to December 31st, 1912, are as eloquent as they are simple They read as follows :—

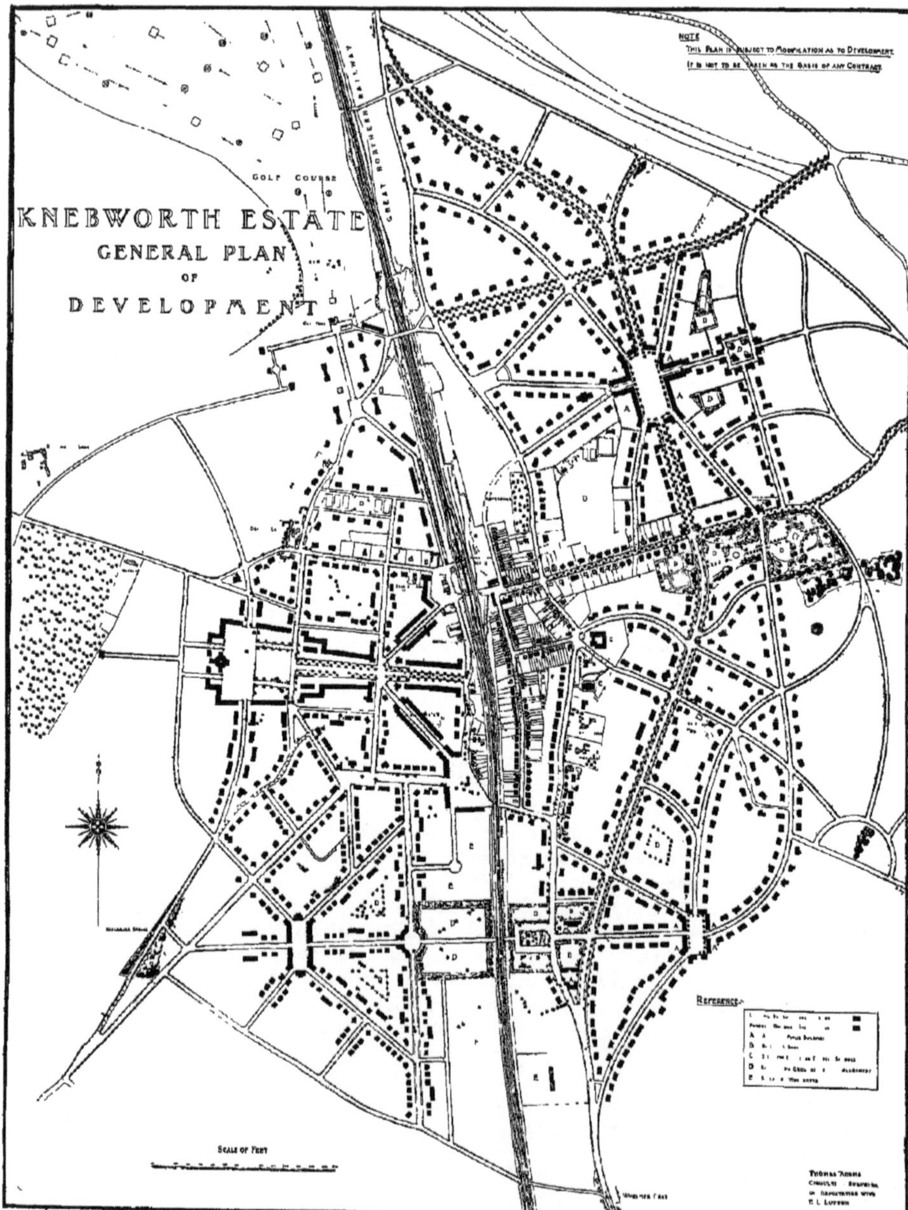

KNEBWORTH ESTATE
GENERAL PLAN
OF
DEVELOPMENT
GOLF COURSE
GREAT NORTHERN RAILWAY
NOTE
THIS PLAN IS SUBJECT TO MODIFICATION AS TO DEVELOPMENT.
IT IS NOT TO BE TAKEN AS THE BASIS OF ANY CONTRACT.
REFERENCE
SCALE OF FEET
THOMAS ADAMS
E. L. LUTYENS

Total number of of sanitary dwellings erected 2,663
Erected prior to 1897 629
Erected since 1911 2,034
(*These are for labouring classes, and they are reserved for the dishoused*).
Death-rate—Declined from 60 to 27 per 1,000.
Typhus Fever—Once never absent; in 1910, not a case.
Tuberculosis—Declined from 4 to 1 9 per 1,000.
Typhoid—In 1896, 1,300 cases; in 1911, 200 cases.
Police Prosecutions—Have fallen 50 per cent

The rents paid do not cover the charges involved by the public expenditure The deficiency is made by striking a rate of 2½d in the £. It is estimated that the ratepayers, if re-housing had not been carried out, would be paying a rate of 5d. in the £ in order to cover the cost of increased inspection, police prosecutions, extra Poor Law rate, and all the other charges that fall upon a city which neglects to deal with its slums

The cash saving to Liverpool under the re-housing policy is estimated at £65,000, or double the cost of providing decent homes for the slum dwellers

LONDON COUNTY COUNCIL DWELLINGS.

Some idea of the magnitude of the work undertaken by the London County Council in the housing of the working classes is shown by the fact that the accommodation provided on March 31st, 1913, was over nine thousand tenements, and nearly two thousand cubicles, with a population of 55,571 people and bringing in a gross annual rental of nearly £220,000 Besides this, accommodation for a further 11,726 persons is in course of provision. The capital cost is £3,400,000. The yearly receipts amount to £225,000 The return upon the cost varies considerably, the return on some estates being as high as nine per cent This is all the result of twenty years' work

The first housing schemes for London were started by the Metropolitan Board of Works, though, owing in some measure to defective legislation, it was some years before anything was done. The first houses to be erected were on the Boundary street area, which, as far beforehand as the year 1839, had been reported upon adversely In 1890 there was a death-rate of forty per thousand over the area. Accommodation for 5,525 persons was completed in March, 1900, and opened by the late King Edward, then Prince of Wales.

The greater part of the Council's work has been in block buildings, but the more recent ventures have been conceived on better lines and some of the estates provide exce'lent examples of housing. The Totterdown Estate at Tooting and the White Hart Lane Estate at Tottenham provide welcome change from the ordinary monotonous housing of the district and an architectural effect has been introduced into the grouping with pleasing results while the latest estate of all, the Old Oak Lane, has provided an opportunity for Garden Suburb lay-out as well as for architectural treatment of the houses.

Tooting Estate is 38¾ acres in extent, costing £1,150 an acre. The cottages are two-storey buildings, in terraces of not more than twenty, and there are no back additions. The houses are 31.81 to the acre and the average cost is as follows Five-roomed cottage, £282 17s ; four-roomed cottage, £240 14s., three rooms and box room, £225 17s.; three-roomed cottage, £190 13s.

The accommodation provided is as follows —

48 two-room cottage flats at rents 6s. 6d. per week.
625 three-room cottages at rents 6s 6d. to 9s. per week
208 three-room and box room cottages at rents 9s. to 10s. per week.
205 four-room cottages at rents 9s. to 11s. per week.
175 five-room cottages at rents 10s 6d to 13s. 6d. per week.

1,261 tenements accommodating 8,788 persons

The White Hart Lane Estate consists of 222 acres, which cost £400 an acre At present nearly fifty acres are developed, and there is a central feature of over three acres known as Tower Gardens, which was secured by a gift from Lord Swaythling 781 cottages with accommodation for 6,202 people have been completed and 105 were in March last in course of erection The majority are fitted with baths The houses will be about twenty-five to the acre The average cost is Five-roomed cottage, £245 ; four-roomed cottage, £225 ; three-roomed cottage, £175

The rents charged are :—

Three-roomed houses 6s. 6d. to 8s. per week
Four-roomed ,, 8s. 6d. to 8s. 9d per week.
Five-roomed ,, 9s. 3d. to 13s per week.

The Old Oak Estate at Hammersmith is one of the most interesting Municipal housing schemes in the country A small portion only is at present being developed Fifty-two dwellings have been provided with a population of 345 people, the rents being :—

Two-roomed tenements 4s 6d to 5s per week
Three-roomed tenements 6s 6d. to 7s 6d per week.
Four-roomed tenements 8s 6d to 10s 6d per week.
Five-roomed tenements 12s per week.

The building has taken the form of squares and crescents surrounding open grass spaces, and on this estate the Council has put into force a scheme for enabling tenants to purchase leases of their houses on the payment of a deposit of £5 and to make equal payments for the first fifteen, twenty or twenty-five years, sufficient to repay the amount expended. It is estimated that the total extra weekly cost to the lessee if he wishes to pay for the building in fifteen years will be from 3s 3d to 4s. for a four-roomed cottage rented at 10s 6d. a week, and from 4s 2d to 4s. 10d for a five-roomed cottage, rented at 12s. 6d. a week If the twenty years' period be chosen the increased weekly cost will be from 1s. 9d. to 2s. 4d for a four-roomed cottage, and 2s. 3d. to 2s. 10d. for a five-roomed cottage. If the lessee chooses the twenty-five years' period, he will purchase the cottage for a charge approximately equal to the ordinary rent

MACHYNLLETH GARDEN VILLAGE.

This Garden Village adjoining the old town of Machynlleth, comprises some fifteen acres of delightfully situated land. The estate has been vested in the Welsh Town Planning and Housing Trust, who will hold the freehold—making the roads and supervising development—and lease land to a Co-operative Housing Society (with a Welsh name—"Tregerddi Machynlleth") which has been formed there to do the building The dividend on the ordinary shares is limited to 5 per cent. and the loan stock to 4 per cent. This example is interesting, in that it is an attempt to deal with the housing problem in a small country town, the population of which is not increasing but which has a large number of tumble-down, insanitary, and overcrowded houses in the old parts of the town. The Urban

District Council is taking a great interest in the scheme, and is rendering assistance by allowing narrower roads to be constructed than the by-laws formerly allowed where there is no through traffic. The lay-out plans for the estate and plans for the houses have been prepared by Mr. Alwyn Lloyd, Architect to the Trust

MERTHYR CO-OPERATIVE GARDEN VILLAGE.

At Merthyr a Co-operative Garden Village Society has been formed. Sixteen acres of land have been leased at Penydarren for 999 years, the lessor granting in addition one acre free for a recreation ground. Mr. Raymond Unwin has prepared the plan, which provides for about 170 houses. It is an excellent example of hillside planning, the houses being placed upon the upper side only of narrow roads. The land slopes to the south, and rises to a height of about a thousand feet above sea level. The Garden Village is in close proximity to some of the worst housing in the kingdom, so that its educational value will be very great The work is being supervised by Professor Jevons. The first contract is for thirty-two houses of nine different types, which will be let at rents varying from 5s to 8s 6d. per week exclusive of rates

NEW EARSWICK.

The Garden Village of New Earswick, near to the city of York, owes its origin to the generosity of Mr Joseph Rowntree, who was desirous of making a practical contribution to the housing question With this end in view he founded a Trust, in December, 1904, known as The Joseph Rowntree Village Trust, of which the following clause is vital to the appreciation of the experiment —

> "The object of the said Trust shall be the improvement of the condition of the working classes (which expression shall in these presents include not only artizans and mechanics, but also shop assistants and clerks, and all persons who earn their living wholly or partially, or earn a small income by the work of their hands or their minds, and further include persons having small incomes derived from invested capital, pensions, or other sources) in and around the City of York, and elsewhere in Great Britain and Ireland, by the provision of improved dwellings with open spaces and, where possible, gardens to be enjoyed therewith, and the organisation of village communities, with such facilities for the enjoyment of full and healthy lives as the Trustees shall consider desirable, and by such other means as the Trustees shall, in their uncontrolled discretion, think fit."

The property lies some 2½ miles to the north of York. The rents of the houses vary according to the accommodation provided. Every house contains three bedrooms, a living-room, scullery, larder, coal-house, etc. In this type of house the bath is generally placed in the scullery. It is covered with a hinged lid, and when not being used for bathing purposes forms a useful table. A good garden is attached to every house in the village.

The total area of the estate is 120 acres, of which over twenty-eight have been develloped, and 150 houses have been erected ; ten houses per acre is the maximum number allowed. About five acres has been set aside and developed as open spaces, and some two acres has been reserved for allotment gardens and small holdings. Rents range from 4s 6d. per week to £60 per annum, rates being payable by the tenants to the Flaxton Rural District Council All roads are tree planted and have grass margins. The estate provides excellent examples of the way in which roads should be laid out both in traffic and non-traffic thoroughfares, and its whole appearance—due to Mr. Unwin's oversight—is perhaps the most pleasing of all the schemes mentioned The rents are low, the gardens ample, the cottages attractive and the roads economical. As a concrete object lesson of what a local authority could do under the Town Planning Act it would be hard to beat

NEW ELTHAM.

New Eltham Garden Suburb is one of the schemes in a district of London which is greatly in need of good building examples. Clare College has followed the example of some of the other seats of learning and has offered an estate of 27 acres for development on co-partnership lines. A society has been formed by old members of the College, who have placed the development in the hands of Mr. George L Pepler On the area named 282 houses will be built, and the demand is such that in all probability the whole will be taken up in a very short time Cottages are proposed at rentals of from 5s. 6d. to 7s. a week. A capital of about £70,000 is being raised for building

NEWTON MOOR.

The Newton Moor Estate is situated in Cheshire, but close to Stockport, and therefore closely connected with the Lancashire manufacturing industries In this example there are already in existence several mills and considerable cottage property of the usual crowded type The general lay-out was already determined by the two main roads across the estate before the new plan, prepared by Mr Thomas Adams, was created The leading feature is a wide tree-planted avenue, intersected by open spaces in its course, running parallel to one of the main roads already in existence The estate has not made much progress at present, but when completed it should form an interesting example of what in the future will be characteristic of a large number of suburban schemes—that is, the superimposition of garden suburb planning on a partially developed site

OLDHAM GARDEN SUBURB.

The Oldham Garden Suburb owes its existence largely to the work of Mrs. Higgs, one of the earliest members of the Garden Cities Association The "Beautiful Oldham" movement had given an impulse to the desire for a better mode of living and a better style of home, and despite many difficulties substantial progress has been made Of the 52 acres one-third has been developed by the Oldham Garden Suburb Tenants Ltd. The houses let from 5s 11d a week to £30 a year Houses of a larger type are built for sale as well as for rent The roads have been made with grass margins and are tree planted, and 3 acres are reserved for open spaces The infantile mortality for the last year shows the following vital statistics —*Birth Rate* 42 per 1,000 population *Death Rate*. 59 per 1,000 births. The *General Death Rate* is 10 per 1,000.

PARK LANGLEY.

This scheme is somewhat different from most of the Garden City ventures It is the work of a firm of builder owners who have been working on housing schemes for the last forty odd years. Park Langley is the latest of their ventures, and was started in June, 1909. The houses vary in design considerably, being the work of many different architects The principal feature of the lay-out plan is found in the converging avenues and roads upon a shopping centre, the idea being to group practically all the shops into one area around a circular winter garden. Above, ample accommodation is provided for those who occupy the shops, with large roof gardens The following figures in connection with this scheme may be of interest: area, 700 acres; population, 500; number of houses allowed per ac e, 4, ultimate number of houses, 2,800 Number of houses now erected, 100 Ultimate population, 14,000

PORT SUNLIGHT.

Messrs. Lever Brothers' Model Village on Bromborough Pool, a tributary of the Mersey, is well known all over the world. The land first acquired, in 1888, was only 56 acres in extent, and of this area 24 acres were devoted to business and manufacturing purposes. Now the works and village comprise an area of 440 acres, in the proportion of 217 allotted to factories, wharves and sidings, and 223 to houses, gardens, village institutions and recreation grounds and other open spaces The houses are all picturesque and substantially built by Messrs Lever Brothers as part of a scheme of Prosperity Sharing, and are let (to employees only) at rents just sufficient to cover upkeep and repair. Sir William Lever holds that his Company gets an ample return for this attention to the housing of the work-people, and for the Co-partnership Scheme more recently launched.

The deep ravines of the Bromborough Pool, most of them now filled up where not needed for navigation, practically decided the original plan of the village, and this has since been the subject of interesting central treatment on lines partly suggested by a prize competition of the students of Liverpool University Department of Civic Design The village is peculiarly rich in institutional and public buildings, including two large schools, a church, Gladstone Hall, Hulme Hall, the Auditorium, Technical Institute, Co-partners' Club, Girls' Club, the Bridge Inn, Open-air Bath and Gymnasium, and a Cottage Hospital The total cost of the 223 acres (area of the village itself), to develop and provide all roads, buildings, houses, etc , is £588,000. The annual cost to the firm is £28,608 a year for interest.

ROTHLEY GARDEN SUBURB.

This private scheme has been initiated by a member of the Garden Cities and Town Planning Association, and is providing a good example of development for the district adjoining Rothley station on the main line of the Great Central Railway between Leicester and Loughborough Some of the Architects most successful at Letchworth and Hampstead have been employed An 18-hole golf course and club house has been opened with a membership of about 200. Tennis courts are also provided. It is contemplated ultimately to develop an area of about 250 acres. Building plots vary from 400 square yards to two and three acres. Up to the present time sixty-nine houses have been erected and about 1,000 yards of the roads, which are tree planted and have grass margins, have been taken over by the Local Authority. The development of the estate has been delayed by the restrictions of the local by-laws and the want of proper sewerage facilities , these are now in course of adjustment. The Estate is five miles from Leicester and Loughborough, and the railway station has been put on the Estate.

RUISLIP MANOR.

Development began in January 1912, and there are now 100 houses erected, largely through a cottage company which has been formed for the estate Houses have varied from four to twelve to the acre, and the average for the whole area will be six. The cost of the cheapest houses so far has been £175 each The land tenure is both freehold and leasehold, and the houses are both let and sold, the proprietors building where necessary A mile and a half of new roads has been made, and these have been sewered and gas and water mains laid. The widths of road in use are forty feet and twenty-four feet, the cost being £3 to £8 per yard run, with a further charge for the final making up The roads are well made and are tree planted, with grass margins

Under the Town Planning scheme of the Ruislip-Northwood Urban District Council, special by-laws are applicable to the land, and these will assist in economical development.

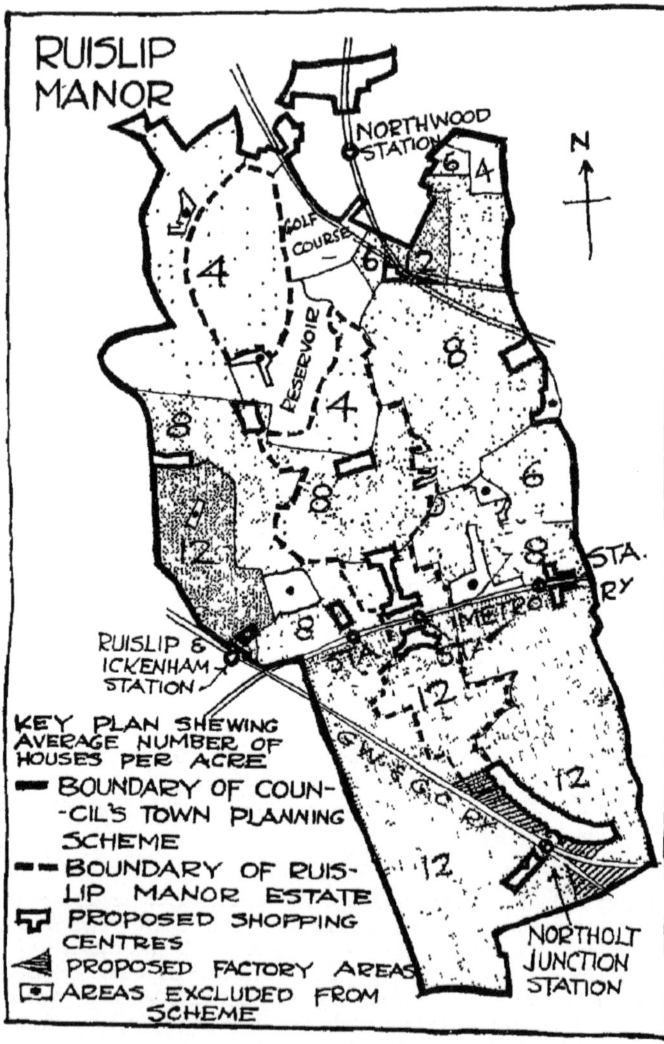

This illustrates both the area of the Ruislip-Norwood Town Planning Scheme, one of the largest in the country, and also the Ruislip Manor Estate situated in the middle. The figures refer to open spaces and unbuilt-on areas

One-tenth of the total area will be reserved as open space, and provision is made for allotments and small holdings. Under the scheme, five acres constitutes a land unit, and the Company is at liberty to group the houses in one land unit upon one portion, provided not more than twenty are put upon one acre and the remainder of the land is left as open space. This allows of the houses being grouped for architectural effect, and provides for economy in roadmaking, etc

The cost of development has varied from £200 to £500 per acre. There are six railway stations close to the estate, and, being quite adjacent to London, the prospects of success are very encouraging.

SEALAND TENANTS.

Sealand Tenants Ltd, whose forty-eight acres of land is situated just over six miles from Chester, have developed ten acres, and, since August, 1910, have built 108 houses out of the 470 provided for at the rate of ten to the acre Five acres have been set aside for recreation purposes and garden allotments The society has provided its own sewage works, and is making its roads thirty-six feet wide, with eighteen feet carriage ways Nearly a mile of road is at present under construction, with both trees and grass margins Rents range from 4s. 9d. to 8s 6d, the rates, which are extra, being 1s. 10d in the £

SOUTHAMPTON GARDEN SUBURB.

The Southampton Garden Suburb, situated just beyond the boundaries of the city, in the area controlled by the Itchen District Council and Bitterne Rural District Council, dates only from August, 1911 It is a commercial project adopting modern Garden Suburb development The total area available is 136 acres, of which some 5½ have been reserved for open spaces, together with fifteen acres of copse. The size of the minimum plots is restricted to 25 feet by 120 feet It is hoped in time to provide 522 houses for an ultimate population of about 2,600

STIRLING HOMESTEADS LIMITED.

Stirling Homesteads Limited is a Co-partnership group. It differs from the ordinary Garden Suburb Scheme principally in this—that the group lease a farm along with the houses and manage this collectively, through a farm committee employing a farm manager, who is also a member of the group.

The object of this is eventually to reduce the cost of the distribution of milk and dairy produce to a minimum and secure the benefits of this to the group. Also to stand as distributing agent for the produce taken off the allotments by the tenants, thus securing Co-operative marketing.

The housing and farm buildings necessary have been erected to meet the Association's requirements by H M. Office of Woods, and the ground has also been leased on a 31 years' lease to the Association by the same body The experiment is just in its infancy, and it is too soon to say anything definite about its prospects, but many of the initial difficulties have been passed, and it is hoped to overcome successfully the few remaining ones.

Out of a total area of 40 acres, 1½ has been built on, 5 are being used as gardens, and 35 are being farmed. The estate is situate 1½ mile from Stirling, and provision is made for an ultimate population of 200 persons and 40 homes. The maximum dividend is limited to 4 per cent. on loan and 5 per cent. on share capital The enterprise dates from the close of 1910. The rents range from £10 10s to £26, rates 2s 6d. in the £ extra.

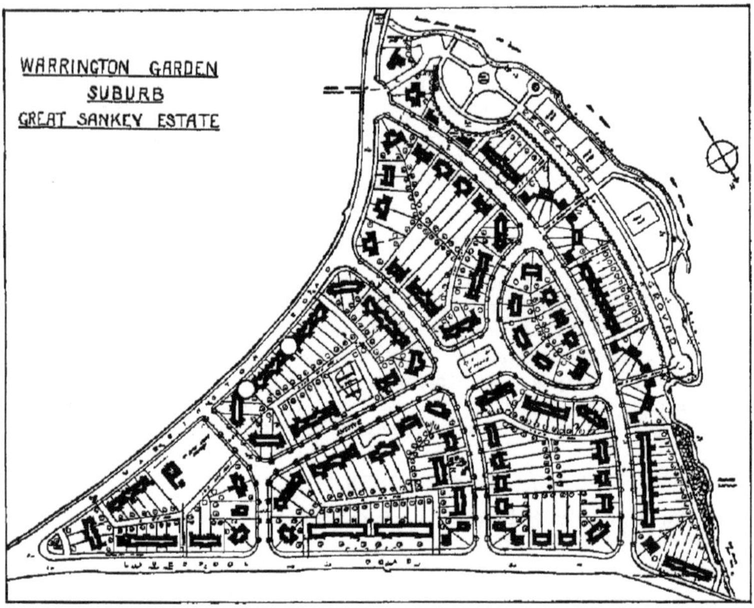
WARRINGTON GARDEN
SUBURB
GREAT SANKEY ESTATE

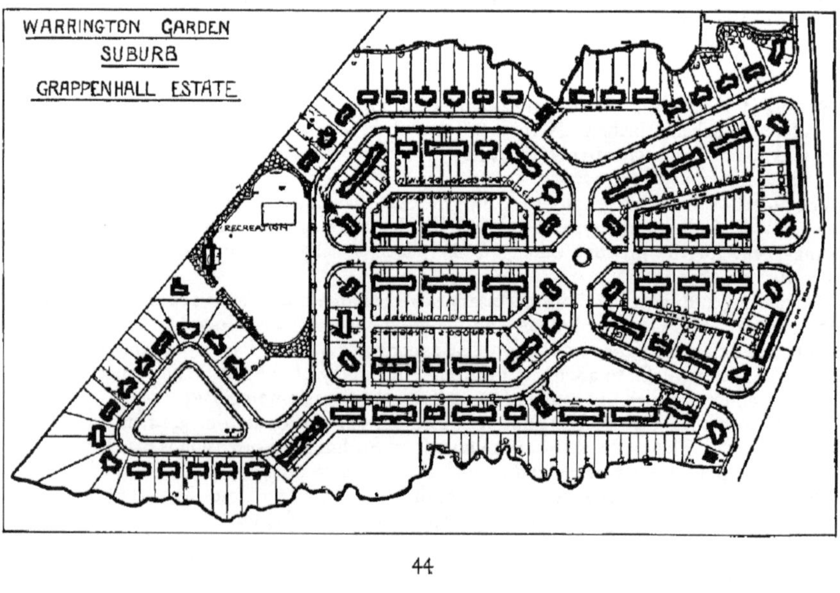
WARRINGTON GARDEN
SUBURB
GRAPPENHALL ESTATE
RECREATION

SUTTON (SURREY) GARDEN SUBURB.

Sutton Garden Suburb Limited has purchased 25½ acres of the Rose Hill estate, Sutton (Surrey), and has an option over another 74½ acres of well-wooded land on the edge of the Downs. Each tenant must be a co-partner, with a maximum holding of £200, and a minimum of £50, which may either be invested straight away or paid by instalments of not less than 5s. a month. Above the £200 investments may be made in loan stock. Shareholding is restricted to tenants and prospective tenants, but loan stock may be applied for by anyone. As 4½ per cent. will be paid on share capital and loan stock, the loan stock having

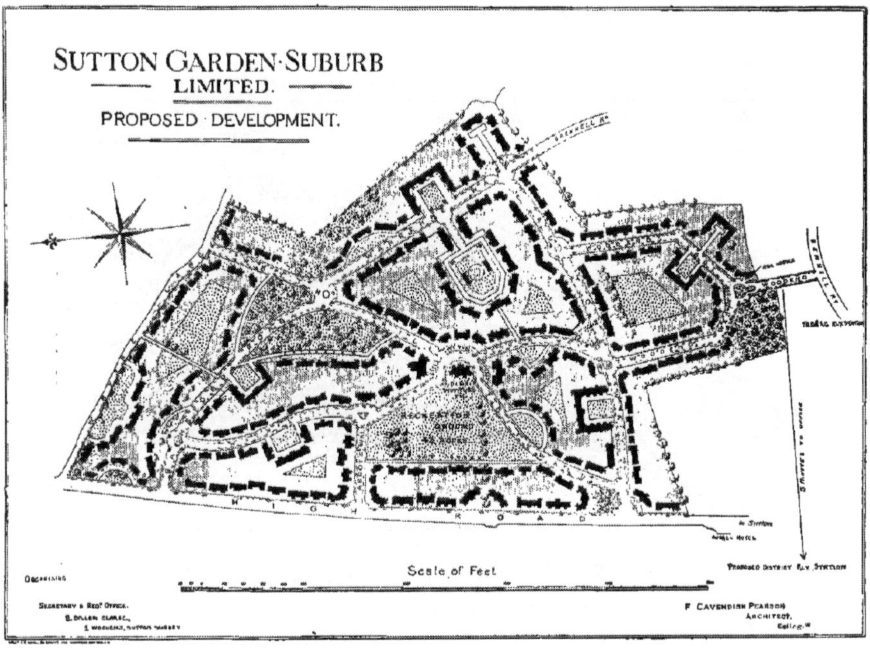

the prior claim but the tenants being more closely associated with management, this should prove an attractive investment. Two loan-stock holders have seats on the Committee. Houses are ten to the acre, and provision is made for extensive recreation grounds and club premises.

WARRINGTON GARDEN SUBURBS LIMITED.

Warrington Garden Suburbs Limited has an outstanding feature of note in that it is the only Company possessing two estates, and which has set out with the definite idea of eventually girdling the town with a ring of Garden Suburbs. It was formed in 1907, and, in the same year, estates were purchased at Great Sankey of about twenty acres, and at Grappenhall of about twenty-two acres. A competition was held with a view to obtaining the best plans for laying them out, and the premiums were won in each case by Messrs. A.

and J Soutar, of Wandsworth The Company is based on the same lines as First Garden City Limited The nominal capital is £20,000, the dividend is restricted to 5 per cent., the number of houses limited to an average of twelve to the acre, and ample open spaces and recreation grounds are carefully provided for. A Society called "Warrington Tenants Limited," was registered in 1908 to assist in the development of the Company's property, and a second Society in 1911, called "Grappenhall Tenants Limited," with similar objects. The progress of the scheme has, hitherto, been somewhat slow; but there are now twenty-four houses on the Great Sankey estate, and twelve at Grappenhall, whilst arrangements for an additional fifteen are practically completed. The cheapest houses on both estates cost about £185; the maximum rent is £30 and the minimum £15 12s per annum. Rates are usually paid by the owners Provision is made for an ultimate number of houses thus: At Great Sankey 240, at Grappenhall 265

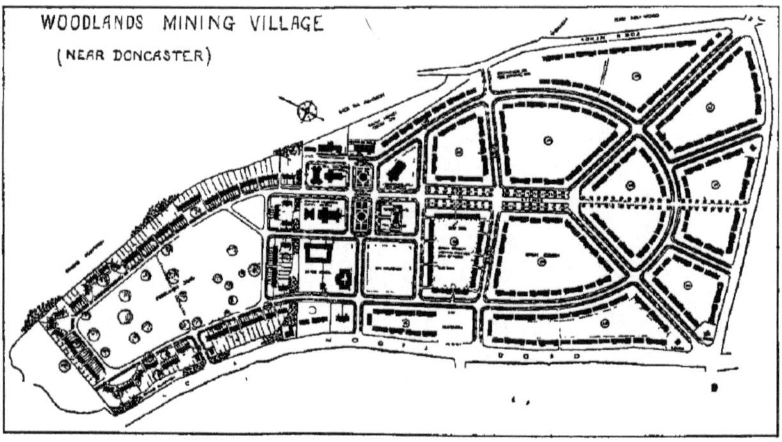

WOODLANDS MINING VILLAGE.

The pretty mining village of Woodlands is one of the most valuable projects which demonstrate the economy and value of town planning. Its total of 653 houses is now complete. The village was commenced in June, 1907, to house the workers of the Brodsworth Main Colliery, largely owing to the determined efforts of Sir A B Markham. The capital required was borrowed on debentures at 5 per cent interest—a high rate for housing purposes—and the basis of the undertaking is that the village shall, at the rentals charged, return 4 per cent on capital after everything, including ground rent, rates and maintenance, is paid. The plan is the work of Mr. Percy B Houfton, of Chesterfield. The estate is of great natural beauty, and adjoins the private residence known as "The Woodlands," which is being converted into a Workmen's Club. Its immediate gardens and the Home Park, in all twenty-one acres, are reserved as recreation grounds.

The village is divided into two sections, linked up by the sites for public buildings and institutions. The portion known as "The Park Site" comprises 121 cottages, which were built in one year, and overlook the Home Park, which contains some magnificent forest trees and is surrounded by a belt of shrubberies. The second portion, "The Field Area," contains 532 houses, built and occupied in fifteen months. The rate of speed, which is too high to ensure good workmanship throughout, was necessitated by unforeseen developments in the coal seam. A main avenue, 120 feet wide, and planted with a quadruple row of trees, is the principal feature of the design, together with numerous open spaces, gardens, an artificial lake covering some four acres, and all the advantages of landscape gardening. Churches, baths, an institute, and co-operative stores are features of the village The rents are as follows: Living-room cottage, 5s 3d ; parlour cottage, with bath in scullery, 6s.; parlour cottage, with bathroom, 6s. 6d.; similar house to the last, but larger, 6s. 9d All rates are included in these figures. The cost of building varied from £156 per house for the smallest to £212 for the largest.

WORCESTER.

A co-partnership society—Worcester Tenants Ltd —has been formed largely through the energies of the Dean, Dr Moore Ede, to start work upon eleven acres of land which has been secured It is hoped to build houses to let at about 5s. a week

WREXHAM TENANTS.

The Welsh Town Planning and Housing Trust Limited has acquired control of some 200 acres of very desirable and well situated land at Acton, adjoining the town of Wrexham, in North Wales. Wrexham is the centre of a large and rapidly developing Coal and Iron district, and in addition to the normal expansion of the town, a new Colliery has just been started near Acton where it is expected that some 3,000 men will be employed in the next two years A Co-partnership Housing Society has been formed locally under the name of Wrexham Tenants Limited to do the building, with Lord Kenyon, Mr. David Davies, M P., and others as Directors, and contracts for the first forty-four houses will be let immediately The Trust will make the roads and supervise the development of the estate. The lay-out plan for the estate includes provision for a village institute, two places of worship, and school, in addition to a liberal provision for open spaces and recreation grounds The District Council has agreed to modified by-laws, which will allow of narrower carriage-ways being provided, in exchange for a greater distance between the houses, and ample open spaces.

YNYSYBWL CO-OPERATIVE GARDEN VILLAGE SOCIETY LIMITED.

The Ynysybwl Co-operative Garden Village Society will be building about fifty-five houses on Lord Plymouth's land at Old Ynysybwl, about three minutes' walk from the upper railway station The site is scarcely three quarters of a mile by road from the Lady Windsor Colliery, where 1,100 men are employed; and it is close to the Mynachdy level, which now employs about 300 men, whilst extensive developments are anticipated. The demand for houses at Ynysybwl is very great, many families being obliged to reside in apa tments who could well afford a house, because there is not one vacant in the town The conditions of overcrowding prevailing at Ynysybwl, and the many abuses to which the extreme shortage of houses has led, have been described in the publication of the Association This Society was formed by the Miners' lodges of the locality, who appointed a joint committee. The Chairman and the Secretary of the Lady Windsor Lodge, with six other miners, were the founders of the Society.

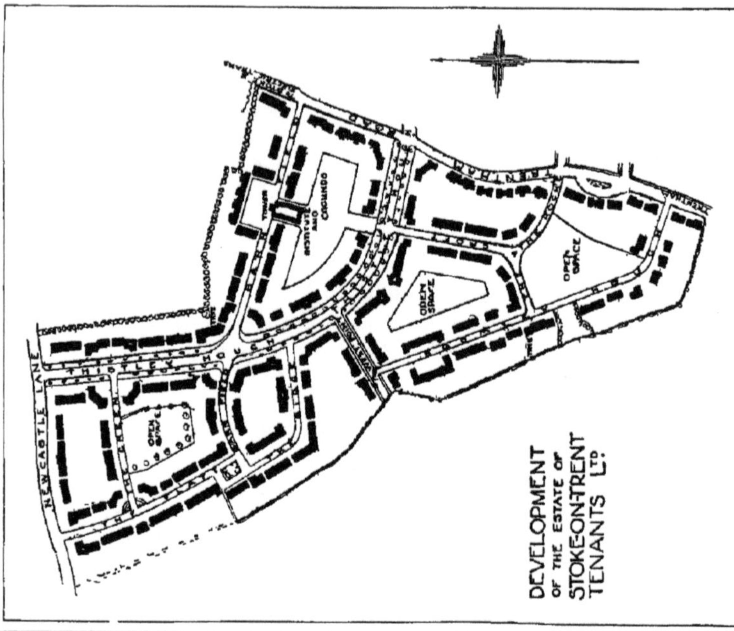
DEVELOPMENT
OF THE ESTATE OF
STOKE-ON-TRENT
TENANTS LTD
NEWCASTLE LANE
OPEN SPACE

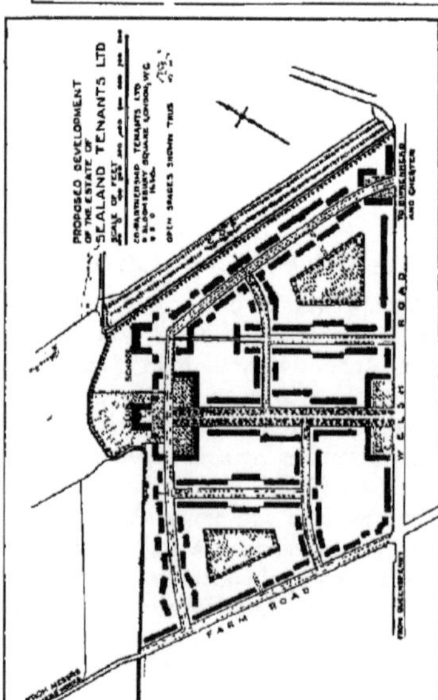
PROPOSED DEVELOPMENT
OF THE ESTATE OF
SEALAND TENANTS LTD
WELSH ROAD
FARM ROAD

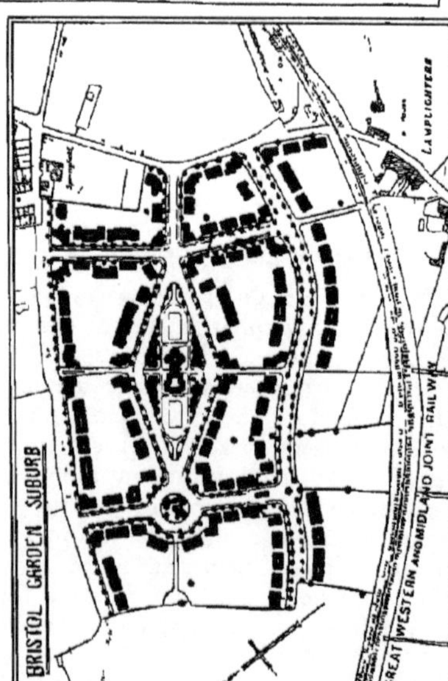
BRISTOL GARDEN SUBURB
GREAT WESTERN AND MIDLAND JOINT RAILWAY
LAMPLIGHTERS

CO-PARTNERSHIP HOUSING

TENANT CO-OPERATORS LIMITED

The forerunner of co-partnership in housing was the Tenant Co-operators Ltd , which is still in existence at Red Lion Square. This organisation was founded in 1888 by Mr Benjamin Jones, then manager of the London branch of the Co-operative Wholesale Society The Rules were prepared by a sub-committee of which, among others, Mr (now Sir) H. J Vansittart Neale, Mr J. J Dent, Mr. Walter Hazell, the late Mr Francis William Buxton, the Hon. T. A. Brassey, Sir H. Lawrence, Mr H W L Roscoe, and the Rev. T. G Gardner were members, and under the guidance of the late Mr E V. Neale and the late Mr J C. Gray (of the Co-operative Union). The rules and prospectus thus prepared have been in operation without any variation in principle from that time until now, and have formed the basis of all the tenant societies established since. Mr Howard Hodgkin was the honorary secretary.

The object of the promoters was to demonstrate the possibilities of the principle and to advocate the formation of similar societies throughout the country. Little or no developments, however, took place until the very remarkable public interest and enthusiasm in housing was aroused by Mr. Howard's scheme for Garden Cities, since when the idea of the combination of the tenant ownership system with the Garden City or Garden Suburb policy has made the establishment of societies so attractive and successful

The Tenant Co-operators Ltd established, either by purchase or erection, five estates at Upton Park, Penge, Camberwell, East Ham, and Epsom The total value of the properties at the present time is £28,670 ; £3,327 has been written off for depreciation The share and loan stock capital stands at £13,969, in addition to which loans from the Public Works Commissioners and other bodies, amounting to £9,841, have been secured The fundamental principle of permitting tenants to become shareholders by the holding of one £1 share, such holding entitling them to a vote equally with any other shareholders, irrespective of the amount of value of the capital held, has been continued throughout the existence of the Society. In this respect other societies have made considerable departure The capital holding of tenants in other societies is usually much larger, and quite recently, in many copartnership societies, the voting power of tenants has been either restricted or removed entirely. The net profits realised by the Tenant Co-operators Ltd , for the whole period of twenty-five years, after payment of all charges, expenses, depreciation, and interest upon loans, deposits, and loan stock, has worked out at 6.7 per cent upon the amount of share capital. For 1912 it was 8.3 per cent. Interest upon share capital being limited by rule, however, to 4 per cent., the surplus profits have been distributed in dividends to tenants, rising to as much as 2s. 6d. in the £.

CO-PARTNERSHIP TENANTS LIMITED

One of the most striking features of the modern movement for better housing has been the successful application of the co-partnership principle Beginning as recently as 1901 Co-partnership Housing has already made history. Under the inspiration of Mr Henry Vivian co-partnership tenants societies have been formed in various parts of the country and are in course of formation in British speaking countries across the seas. Many are now federated in the Co-partnership Tenants Ltd, a society that has secured public confidence in the movement to a degree that would otherwise have been impossible There are now fourteen societies in membership. In 1904 the cost value of their land and buildings was £17,308 ; already it is a million and a quarter sterling, and the estimated value of the houses when the estates now being developed are completed is £3,450,000 The headquarters are at 6, Bloomsbury Square, London, W.C, where an efficient organisation with trading, architectural, publishing, and other departments has been built up to render substantial assistance to the federated societies.

At present 900 acres are under development by the societies associated with Co-partnership Tenants Ltd, and the following figures concerning the rentals of the property already built are of interest .—

Below 6s. weekly	640	Brought forward ..	2,553
From 6s. and below 8s.	921	From 12s. and below 15s ..	168
„ 8s. „ 10s. ..	558	„ 15s and up to 20s ..	79
„ 10s. „ 12s . ..	434	Over £52 per annum . .	155
Carried forward .. .	2553	Grand total	2,955

The strong position which the Co-partnership Tenants societies have attained may be gathered from the fact that eight co-partnership societies in federation which have practically completed their building operations and having property to the value of £797,345 have not only no dwelling of any kind to let, but have "waiting lists" of applicants.

The following particulars show the growth of the Society's Capital, and the extent to which the Society has aided the movement in raising Capital

On December 31st, 1912, the Society's Capital consisted of :—

	£		£	
Shares of £10 each . ..	68,160	Increase during the year	6,350	
Loan Stock	198,368	„ „ „	60,584	
Loans	70,317	„ „ „	30,801	
	£336,845			97,735

A typical new street of an industrial town. The houses are built forty or more to the acre, and in this instance the frontages are 12 feet only.

A street at Hampstead Garden Suburb.

Bristol Garden Suburb Cottages costing £150 each.

Hampstead, showing a Common Green.

A Crescent, showing Common Green.

Bournville. The Shopping Centre.

During the year the Society, as Agent, also raised direct for the various Societies in membership :—

	£	£
Shares	1,810	
Loan Stock ..	21,768	
On Mortgage ..	97,575	
		121,153
Total amount raised in 1912		218,888
From June, 1907 (when the Society was registered), to December 31st, 1911, the total sum raised direct in Shares, Loan Stock, and on Mortgage for the various Societies was	651,269	
There was invested in Co-partnership Tenants Limited up to the same date	239,110	
		890,379
Grand Total		£1,109,267

Continued progress was made in 1913, the total paid-up capital of Co-partnership Tenants Ltd on September 1st being :—Shares, £76,960 ; Loan Stock, £224,520 ; a total of £301,480.

In the development of the work the Co-partnership Tenants Housing Council has rendered considerable assistance, and under its guidance much of the educational and social work is fostered on the various estates—the activities being chronicled in *Co-partnership*, the penny monthly magazine of the movement. It also organises the Co-partnership Festival which is held annually on one or other of the co-partnership estates—Ealing, 1912, and at Hampstead, in July, 1913—at which a Flower Show, Choral Contests, a Pageant, displays by children living on the estate, and other features demonstrate the advantages of these co-partnership suburbs both in their effect on the individual and on the general welfare of the community.

Below, particulars are given of the estates affiliated to Co-partnership Tenants Ltd., that fact alone being an assurance of the exercise of forethought and prudence in development. Details which are common to all estates have been omitted for the sake of brevity. In every case, of course, the owners are a society of public utility, the maximum dividends being 5 per cent

ANCHOR TENANTS LTD. (LEICESTER).

The Anchor Tenants Ltd., Leicester, own forty-eight acres a mile and a half from the boundary of the town ; and since a start was made in 1908 eighty-four houses and three shops have been built, and there is a population of about 360 residents. Ten houses are allowed to the acre. The vital statistics for the estate are very striking ; there was only one death in four years, and the birth-rate is thirty per thousand. Rents range from 6s. to 10s. 9d including rates, which are at 4s. 8d. in the pound. The streets are tree-planted with grass margins. Roads have been formed and sites plotted for another sixty houses. Provision has been made for a larger playing ground, comprising about three acres, part of which has been levelled and re-turfed for a cricket pitch.

BRENTHAM GARDEN SUBURB (EALING).

The Brentham Garden Suburb, as the estate of the Ealing Tenants Ltd. is now called, is the oldest of the ventures connected with Co-partnership Tenants Ltd. Various portions of land have been acquired since 1902, and the estate now consists of sixty-three acres. Its easy access to London, the new Brentham Station having been opened close at hand, gives every reason for expectation that the whole area will soon be built upon The roads

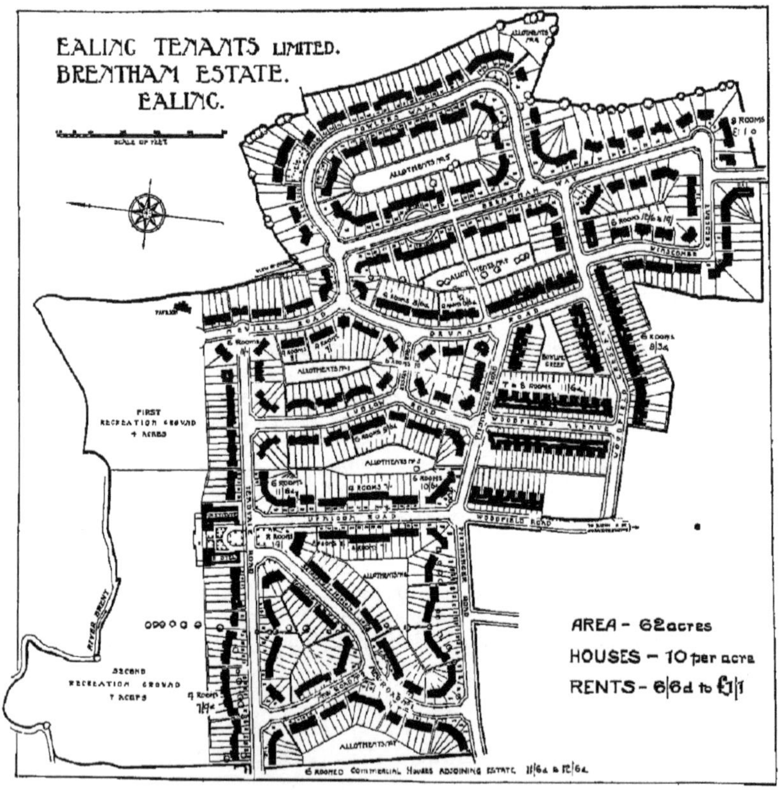

are forty feet wide, and all are tree planted. At present 500 houses are built out of 700 anticipated, and there is a population of about 2,000 out of the three to four thousand expected. The houses are limited to twelve to the acre The maximum rent is 21s. and the minimum 6s. 6d., the rates, which are extra, being 6s. 8d in the £. A block of twenty-four small flats has also been completed and tenanted, with rents from 6s. 6d. per week inclusive of rates, taxes, and lighting. The Institute, opened by H.R.H. the Duke of Connaught, provides excellent facilities for social intercourse. It contains a large billiard room, hall for social purposes, reading room and library; and connected with it, the Society has reserved twelve acres of recreation grounds. These facilities are much appreciated by the residents, and full advantage is taken of them Other open spaces are reserved for additional gardens, etc.

BURNAGE

Manchester Tenants Ltd have completed their Burnage estate of eleven acres, their 136 houses giving accommodation to 500 people Rents vary from 5s. 3d. to 11s. 6d., the rates, which are extra, being 8s. 4d. in the £ The society has made its roads of twenty-two feet and eighteen feet, and has planted the whole of these with trees and provided grass margins. Application is now being made to the local authority for them to take over the roads.

FALLINGS PARK TENANTS.

Fallings Park Garden Suburb Tenants have so far developed 8½ acres of their estate, which is one-and-a-half miles from Wolverhampton At the rate of twelve houses to the acre, seventy-five have been erected since June, 1907. The rents range from 4s. 6d. to 10s. inclusive. The rates are 9s. 4d. in the £. Thirty-six feet roads are in use, and these are planted with trees

GARDEN CITY TENANTS.

The Garden City Tenants Ltd. was the society whose inception led to that combination of garden city principles with co-partnership methods which has revolutionised both movements, and has brought into being the enormous structure of Co-partnership Tenants Ltd. Thirty-nine acres have been developed, and 322 houses providing accommodation for 1,600 people Twelve houses to the acre are allowed; but the generous garden space provided and the charming open greens, which are such a feature of the estate, reduce the total number of houses to 322 The rents range from 4s. 6d a week to £61 a year, rates, which are 4s 9d. in the £, being extra

GRETA HAMLET.

Greta Hamlet, Keswick, is the property of Derwentwater Tenants Ltd, who started with 2½ acres in 1909, and have practically covered this area. The roads are made twenty-four feet and twelve wide, and are planted with grass and garden margins.

HAMPSTEAD HEATH EXTENSION TENANTS LIMITED.

Hampstead Heath Extension Tenants Ltd. was registered on the 25th March, 1912, and was formed to develop some of the finest sites on the Hampstead Garden Suburb, overlooking and bordering on the eighty acres of the Hampstead Heath Extension. On this area houses of varying rentals are being erected, mostly of the larger type. Some of these houses have frontages to the Heath while overlooking the Hampstead Golf Course and Turners Wood at the rear. The land is situated within a few minutes' walk of the old Spaniard's Inn, and other historical spots associated with the neighbourhood.

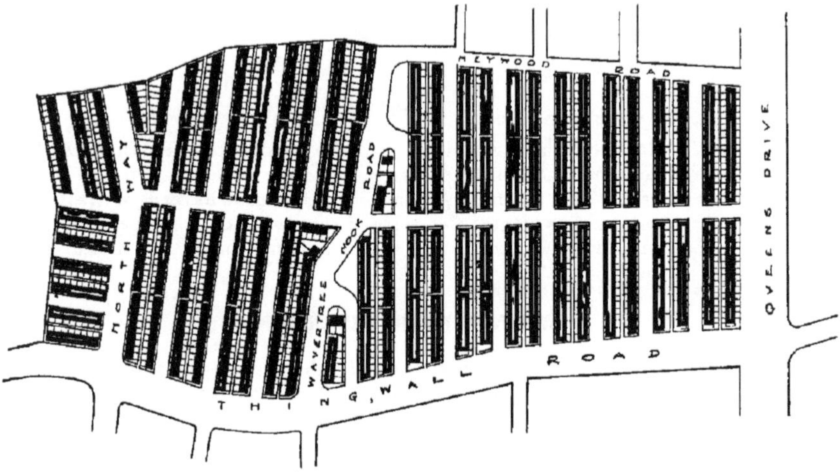

TWENTY-FIVE ACRES OF LIVERPOOL GARDEN SUBURB AS IT MIGHT HAVE BEEN

The plan shows how the land could have been laid out to comply with the minimum requirements of the Liverpool Corporation's Acts, with 41 houses per acre.

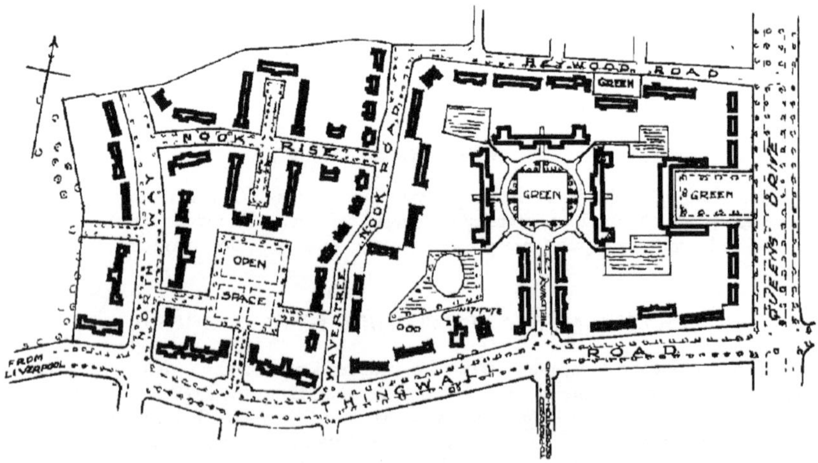

TWENTY-FIVE ACRES OF LIVERPOOL GARDEN SUBURB AS IT IS.

The first part of the Estate, showing eleven houses per acre.

THE HAMPSTEAD TENANTS SOCIETIES.

Hampstead Tenants Ltd has perhaps had the greatest amount of publicity directed to it owing to the visit of the King and Queen and other members of the Royal Family, as well as statesmen from all parts of the world. The first two Co-partnership Societies formed on the Hampstead Garden Suburb have developed the whole of their area and now an additional 380 acres have been taken for development by kindred societies

Hampstead Tenants Ltd. started in May, 1907, and its first houses were opened by Sir William Treloar (then Lord Mayor of London) in October of the same year. The buildings comprise 271 houses, a block of shops with flats over, and fifty-four Homes for Old People, the whole population being about 1,200 The rents of the Homes are as low as 3s. 3d. per week, and the houses are let, mostly at weekly rentals, from 6s upwards.

Second Hampstead Tenants Ltd has developed its thirty-nine acres (exclusive of roads and common open spaces), having 377 houses, a block of shops with flats, seventy-six workmen's flats, and another block of larger flats, altogether housing about 1,900 people. This Society commenced operations in the autumn of 1909 and, like the Hampstead Tenants Ltd, has the whole of its property fully let. Rents range from 5s. 9d. per week to £130 per annum, exclusive of rates.

HARBORNE TENANTS.

Harborne Tenants, Birmingham, have now developed the whole of their fifty-four acres, which is situated only 2½ miles from the centre of the city. Since September, 1907, 499 houses have been built, with a present population of 1,600. The character of the site presented great difficulties on this estate, and the way they have been overcome proves the soundness of the idea Nine acres of land have been given up to allotments and playgrounds. The vital statistics show a death-rate of four per thousand, and birth rate of forty, and there has been no infantile mortality from the commencement With rates at 8s 2d in the £, houses with from one-tenth of an acre of garden are let as cheaply as 4s per week, including rates, and the rentals go to £40 a year without rates. Two and one-eighth miles of roads have been made, and have been planted with trees and have grass margins, while the estate has provided 2¼ miles of gas and water mains. The local authority has so far taken over 694 yards of road

LIVERPOOL GARDEN SUBURB.

Liverpool Garden Suburb Tenants Ltd have so far the biggest co-partnership estate, having taken from Lord Salisbury 180 acres of his Childwall estate, of which thirty acres are being proceeded with Since July, 1910, 260 houses have been built, from ten to twelve to the acre, and it is anticipated that this number will grow to 1,800, housing nearly 7,000 people. One acre in every ten is set aside for open spaces. The rents range from 5s 7d. a week to £31 a year, the rates, which are extra, being 8s. 5d. in the £. The roads are of varied construction. They are planted with trees and with grass margins, and the widths vary between thirty-six, fifty, sixty and eighty feet. In addition to the buildings a recreation ground containing bowling green and tennis courts has been laid out, and a children's playground has been provided. The estate has appealed strongly to those anxious to see better conditions of housing in Liverpool, and in his annual report the Building Surveyor for the City of Liverpool has testified to the advantages of the Liverpool Garden Suburb and said that "the beneficial effect on the character and well-being of the people who live in such delightful surroundings, in which the provision of sunlight and pure air, and other sanitary necessities of healthful living are so admirably secured, must be incalculable"

OAKWOOD TENANTS LIMITED.

The latest of the Co-partnership Tenant Societies on the Hampstead Garden Suburb is that of the Oakwood Tenants Ltd, registered in January, 1913 This Society has already over 100 houses in hand and will continue the policy of the Hampstead Tenants Ltd. and the Second Hampstead Tenants Ltd, of building houses at rents ranging from 7s. per week to £80 per annum exclusive of rates The land acquired occupies some of the pleasantest sites on the fringe of the two woods which have recently been included in the Suburb area.

SEVENOAKS TENANTS.

Sevenoaks Tenants Ltd. has its land split up in three different parts of the town; but on the 6½ acres which it has been able to acquire some excellent housing has been provided. A start was made in 1904 and the area is now developed, eighty houses having been built About an acre of woodland playground near 34 houses has been set aside, and land is hired close by for small holdings. Rents are from 4s. 9d. to 12s. 6d, rates inclusive. Additional land has been obtained at Kemsing upon which six houses have been erected, and efforts are being made to do something for the neighbouring villages.

STOKE-ON-TRENT TENANTS.

Stoke-on-Trent Tenants Ltd owns 38 acres, of which ten have been developed. This Potteries Garden Village, close to the newly-formed borough of Stoke-on-Trent, is providing an excellent example of the co-operation of all sections of the community. Since April, 1910, about ninety-five houses have been built at ten to the acre. One-tenth of the estate is set aside for open spaces, and allotments are provided The rents are from 5s a week to £60 a year, rates being 10s The widths of the roads, all of which have trees and grass margins, vary from twenty-four to seventy feet. The estate as already planned has been adopted into and forms part of the proposed town planning scheme prepared for the Borough Council by Mr. A Burton, A M.I.C E, the Borough Surveyor of Stoke-on-Trent, which includes a large area adjoining the estate and extending from Harpfield to Trent Vale. The main avenue through the estate, which is being constructed seventy feet wide between the boundaries and 100 feet between the houses, will be linked up with the main arteries of the scheme.

RURAL CO-PARTNERSHIP.

In order to promote Co-partnership housing in rural districts a Rural Co-partnership Association has been formed with similar objects to the Co-partnership Housing Council. A business department has been formed, known as the Rural Co-partnership Housing Trust Limited, with which are affiliated several societies engaged in building, these being Datchet, Bucks, 30 acres; Otford (Kent), 160 acres; Petersfield (Hants), 33 acres; Somersham (Hunts), 17½ acres; Hadleigh (Suffolk), 7½ acres; Budleigh (Devon), 4 acres. There are other societies in process of formation as far apart as Bridge-of-Weir and St Mawes, Cornwall.

One of the societies has put up a pair of brick cottages at a total cost of £232, including all extras, pumps, paths, fencing, gates, and fees for plans and supervision. The accommodation consists of a living-room 12 ft. by 12 ft, scullery 8 ft by 7 ft., pantry 6 ft by 3 ft, and three bedrooms, one on the ground floor alternately usable as a parlour. The largest bedroom is 12 ft. by 12 ft., and the smallest 10½ ft. by 8½ft. A novel arrangement was made with the contractor, under which his percentage fees, instead of increasing with the amount of the contract, increased according to the extent to which he was legitimately able to lessen the cost

The Council is following the true method of co-partnership and the tenants take up three £1 shares, paid for by instalments of a penny a week, with a preliminary payment of 1s. a share, and it is interesting to notice that security of tenure is given to the tenant, and this tenancy passes to his family after him so long as the conditions of membership are fulfilled. This meets one of the difficulties often raised in connection with co-partnership tenancy and does away with the fear of a tenant being victimised in consequence of some temporary difference of opinion.

BRIDGE OF WEIR.

At Bridge of Weir, a town of some 2,500 population near Glasgow, having one or two factories, the intention is to afford the industrial employees a much needed opportunity of getting into touch with garden and agricultural environment. The housing conditions of many wage earners in Scotland are of a primitive kind, and it is hoped that once a model society is successfully established in Lanarkshire, the example set will be followed elsewhere.

DATCHET.

This society has now nearly completed its building of twenty-eight cottages, and some of the tenant members are in. All the land is under cultivation. There are some seventy allotment tenants, additionally to the house tenants The total cost of land and cottages will work out at nearly £8,000. Lord Rothschild is President of the society, which has powers under its rules to form a co-operative trading society and probably at an early date will add this development to the existing organisation

HADLEIGH.

The society formed for this district has purchased its land and is building its first cottages The inclusive cost per cottage, counting all extras, will be £140. They will be built in pairs and have not less than a quarter of an acre of land attached. Rents will be 4s 3d. inclusive of rates, and the accommodation will include five rooms, scullery and pantry. The society has twelve cottages for its first scheme, the estimated cost of land and building being £2,000.

OTFORD.

This society has made much progress and is well forward with its building programme. Various tenant members are already housed and the estate has been subdivided into holdings, and is under varied cultivation. The brook has been utilised for a water supply on the ram system. The services of a Danish agriculturist have been secured to exemplify on the estate Danish expert methods of small farming. Schemes for an agricultural co-operative society and a credit bank are under consideration.

PETERSFIELD.

The society has purchased thirty-three acres of suitable and well situated land, and is about to build for its first scheme eighteen cottages, which are already bespoken by tenant members. Each cottage will have not less than a quarter of an acre of land as garden. The estimated cost of land and cottages totals £6,000 Lord Selborne is President.

ST. MAWES.

The scheme at St. Mawes, Cornwall, is to meet the need of fishermen and others of the labouring classes for better cottages with some land attached Owing to the increase in the number of visitors to this fishing village there is a danger of the poorer inhabitants having their cottage accommodation curtailed.

SOMERSHAM.

Seventeen and a quarter acres of good fruit land have been purchased, and building begun The contract price for the cottages in pairs, including all extras, paths, wells, fencing, etc, is £134 5s. Not less than half an acre of land will go with each cottage All the tenants earn their living by agricultural work. The society will continue building until the demand for cottages and land is met, and if necessary, steps will subsequently be taken to secure further land. The estimated cost of land and houses for the first scheme is £3,300.

THE CO-OPERATIVE MOVEMENT AND HOUSING REFORM

It is somewhat remarkable that the wave of housing enthusiasm that is sweeping throughout the country has to a very large extent left almost entirely untouched a movement supposed to be progressive in character.

The co-operators of the United Kingdom, with their unrivalled and compact organisation, their vast resources of capital, and exceptional facilities for gauging the housing requirements of their 2½ million members, have, comparatively speaking, done very little towards meeting the needs of their members in this respect. The housing that has been undertaken falls very far short of what the Garden City and Garden Suburb movement claims as a standard of working-class housing, and lacks the foresight and comprehensiveness that one might have expected

The latest statistics published are as follows :—

Co-operative Societies who have building departments	413
Money lent to members for the purchase of their houses ...	£6,532,000
Number of houses so built	32,000
Money spent by Societies on houses built and afterwards sold to members	£1,232,000
Number of houses so built and sold	5,577
Money spent by Societies on building houses let to members ..	£1,839,000
Number of houses so let	8,530
Total—46,707 houses at a capital cost of	£9,603,000

The Co-operative Garden City Committee, of Halton House, Holborn, E C, is an organisation of Co-operators formed in 1908 for the purpose of improving the housing conditions in the Co-operative movement, and giving technical advice and assistance in the matter of capital raising, planning of estates, etc, to those societies desirous of setting on foot housing undertakings of an improved character One of the principal members of the organisation is Mr. Aneurin Williams, Chairman of First Garden City Ltd., while Mr F. W Rogers, hon secretary, has a wide inside knowledge of the movement on both its propagandist and practical sides.

In the first few years of its existence the committee's energies were largely confined to work of a propagandist character, but lately one or two definite garden suburb schemes have been initiated that are a distinct improvement on typical co-operative housing undertakings

The Co-operative Garden City Committee are hoping that five or six other co-operative societies with whom they are in negotiation, and to whom they have supplied schemes of estate planning, will soon be engaged in the building of co-operative garden suburbs, which will both act as a stimulus to the co-operative movement and help to remove the reproach of bad housing that seems to have fallen upon it.

CHIPPING NORTON.

A scheme of development for a twelve acre Co-operative Housing Scheme at Chipping Norton is also in hand which will involve the erection of houses to let at rentals as low as 4s. 6d per week inclusive.

WOKING.

The most recent example is an admirable scheme of nine acres that is being evolved in connection with the Woking Co-operative Society Ltd., and known as the Horsell Estate. Only eight houses will be erected to the acre, and these when built will be let to the members of the Woking Society at rentals ranging from 7s 6d. to 10s per week

Mr. H. Clapham Lander, A.R.I.B.A , the hon advisory architect to the Co-operative Garden City Committee, has been responsible for the plan of development At the present time one-third of the Estate has been developed, with buildings completed and roads made The President of the Local Government Board recently inspected the Garden Suburb and expressed himself favourably towards it When completed, the whole scheme will cost about £20,000, a proportion of the capital required having been obtained from the Co-operative Wholesale Society at $3\frac{3}{4}$ per cent , and the remainder will either be found by the Woking society itself or obtained from the Public Works Loan Commissioners.

THE GARDEN CITY MOVEMENT ABROAD

GERMANY.

So far as the continent of Europe is concerned, Germany has made by far the most substantial progress, thanks to the devoted enthusiasm of the cousins Kampffmeyer and of Adolf Otto, who between them have borne the chief burden of the organisation.

There are difficulties to contend with in Germany which are unknown in England, and, considering these, the progress which has been made is remarkable, and last year's success was very gratifying. One thing which makes the work more difficult is the fact that many of the banks and institutions which lend money on mortgage for the building of ordinary houses will not do so for cottage property, and it is only provincial labourers' insurance institutes (Landesversicherunganstalten) which will lend any considerable sums, up to 75 or even 90 per cent of the value of land and houses These excellent terms are obtained chiefly in the western and southern parts of the country In some of the eastern parts—Berlin, for example—money cannot be obtained because, the flat system being almost universal, cottage property is not considered sufficient security. The Prussian Government, however, will advance money on second mortgage to co-partnership societies, among the members of which must be a good number of officials.

It will be seen, therefore, that, as was found in England, the progress of the movement depends largely on the question of money, but there is also the difficulty that because of the opposition of many landowners to the improved methods of housing the people, most of the Corporations object to the new plans. Nevertheless, in both eastern and western Prussia progress is being made, although only one example exists—that of the Garden Suburb Ratshof, near Konigsberg A number of towns in that district have, however, made application for the travelling exhibition of the Association to be shown in their towns, and as a result of this, preliminary work has been started

Germany suffers perhaps more than England from the unwarranted use of the term Garden City, and there are a number of schemes unconnected with the Association of which it is apparently impossible to obtain particulars. The chief difficulty operating against greater progress is the land difficulty, which often makes it impossible to proceed, and added to this is the road problem. Almost everywhere the municipal authorities insist on wide expensive thoroughfares, even for residential districts, despite the universal testimony of the newer school of Town Planners, who have learnt the lesson of the narrow metalled surfaces adopted at Letchworth and elsewhere. The ideal plans, therefore, have frequently to be abandoned, and for example the requirements at the new Berlin Garden Suburb prevent altogether the erection of labourers' cottages. The Government favours the proposed plan, but can do nothing in face of the corporation, which insists on having the same broad streets as those which carry the traffic of Berlin.

In addition to issuing a monthly magazine (*Gartenstadt*), with a circulation of 5,000 copies, a number of excellent books have been issued, which are among the best literature issued in connection with the whole movement. Each year large parties of municipal representatives, architects, engineers, and educationalists are brought to England to study the movement at first hand

The biggest and the most important of the German schemes is that of Hellerau, near Dresden, in which, in the past four years, nearly eight million marks have been invested. The second big estate is the Garden Suburb, Stockfeld, near Strassburg, a very interesting scheme, which provides also small homes for poorer families. This scheme was made possible by the assistance of the Corporation of Strassburg, which has sold land to the Association cheaply and has guaranteed a sum of two million marks for building purposes. Further, there is the Garden Suburb of Margaretenhohe, near Essen, which may be described as the German Bournville, being conducted under a trust similar to that instituted by Mr. George Cadbury. It was founded by the widow of the late Mr Krupp.

Both Stockfeld and Margaretenhohe are being built by only one architect each, while in Hellerau a number of the best architects in Germany have been assigned certain quarters to plan and build, in order to secure the best result.

A very interesting community on pure co-partnership lines is the Garden Suburb of Wandsbeck, near Hamburg, where an estate has been bought from the Corporation and where already, in the third year, more than 200 houses are ready. The Corporation of Altona, who in the past year has sent its Lord Mayor and a number of officials to England to study the Garden City question, will lease land to the same association for an estate for 30,000 people, and in order to fulfil its programme for the whole district of Hamburg and its environs, the various co-partnership associations have united into one large organisation. For this work the Prussian Government has advanced a good deal of money

After some very hard work, the Garden Suburb of Karlsruhe has begun building operations, and forty houses are inhabited. The same applies to Nurnberg The Mannheim Garden Suburb is being built on municipal land let on lease. The Garden Suburb of Marienbrunn, which is also leasehold on municipal land, will have the first portion completed early in the Spring, when the Leipsig International Building Exhibition will be opened, of which for the summer it will form a part.

During the past year large and small co-partnership associations have been founded, and estates have been secured at Aachen, Bonn, Gera, Hamm, Dortmund, Aschersleben, Liegnitz, Frankfurt-a-O., Halle, Skopau, Thorn, Allenstein, Danzig, etc.

In the case of Munich, where much was hoped for, it has been found impossible to proceed, although a well-wisher gave the Corporation of Munich a sum of 200,000 marks to start It has been found, however, that the questions of incorporation, traffic, sewerage, etc., were too difficult to surmount

A much more important scheme is the Garden Suburb near Berlin, founded by the members of the German Association Committee. 150 acres have been secured. Already in Berlin-Britz a Co-partnership Society is building cottages and small tenements on very expensive ground, where usually the huge German tenements would have been built, and have thereby given a very useful example to the community

Huttenau, near Essen, is of much interest, inasmuch as the two communes of Blankenstein and Welper have given a guarantee to the Insurance Institute for the whole of the capital required, and this is endorsed by the Rural District of Huttenau. In this case both the money for the purchase of the land and for the building of the houses has been advanced.

The following tabulates the estates in Germany:—

Altona (Hamburg).—Provision for 30,000 people. Municipal assistance

Gross-Berlin.—Society three years old. 150 acres secured, and thirty-five houses have been built with the assistance of the Government, which has advanced the necessary money on second mortgage for this first stage. A second sum of M.200,000 has been secured for the second batch of houses.

Güstrow, in Mecklenburg —Existing town of 18,000 inhabitants, largely agricultural Started by a manufacturer (Herr Dettmann) on 3 hectars. To be extended and handed over to the community.

Hellerau, near Dresden.—140 hectars purchased in 1908. 200 dwellings completed, as well as factories and institutions.

Hopfengarten (Magdeburg) —65 morgen After one year 400 inhabitants. System of purchase of freehold by inhabitants, with power of repurchase by society in a number of eventualities.

Huttenau.—Founded 1909 in consequence of the growth of one large firm. 400 morgen. Supported officially by the two communes concerned, who have agreed to the carrying out of one plan 166 houses built in 1910-11

Karlsruhe.—12 hectars. Building begun July, 1911. Forty houses ready.

Marienbrunn (Leipsig).—Land leased by municipality. The first section constitutes part of the Leipsig International Building Exhibition and includes some interesting garden architecture.

Margaretenhöhe.—Started in 1906 An endowment of 1,000,000 marks by Mrs Krupp. 50 hectars for 15,000 to 18,000 inhabitants. Gardens 70 to 300 qm.

Mannheim.—Society founded 1910. Town granted 40 hectars. First groups now ready

München-Perlach.—A project to lay out 80-85 hectars for 12,000 to 13,000 inhabitants.

Neumunster.—100 hectars. To provide houses for well-paid artisans, with four or five rooms at 5,000 to 6,000 marks, with good gardens, the average size of plots being 700 qm. By the spring of 1912, 75 houses completed

Nurnberg.—In 1908 chose 65 hectars of State land. In 1910 began with 4 hectars, having obtained a municipal loan of 20,000 marks; 74 houses now ready.

Ratshof bei Konigsberg.—Society built tenement houses from 1895 to 1906. In 1906 bought 200,000 qm for single houses, of which 51 have been built

Stockfeld (Strassburg).—Scheme initiated by Municipality, which handed over 123,930 qm to a society to develop 170 detached, 280 semi-detached houses Many arrangements for self-government and life of community

Wandsbeck (Hamburg).—Started in 1910. 4½ hectars 150 houses completed by summer, 1912.

Associations have been formed for co-operative housing at Rostock, Tilsit, Plauen, Chemnitz, Bonn, Aachen (Aix la Chapelle), Dortmund, Halle, and Erfurt At Gera a society with a limited dividend is building houses on Garden City lines.

A word should be added as to the most excellent housing work which has been accomplished by the firm of Krupp's for the benefit of their workpeople. Some forty thousand people, all the families of their employees, are housed in the fourteen village settlements provided for them at rents much below those charged in the district and in surroundings superior to anything provided in the German Empire One of the most attractive of

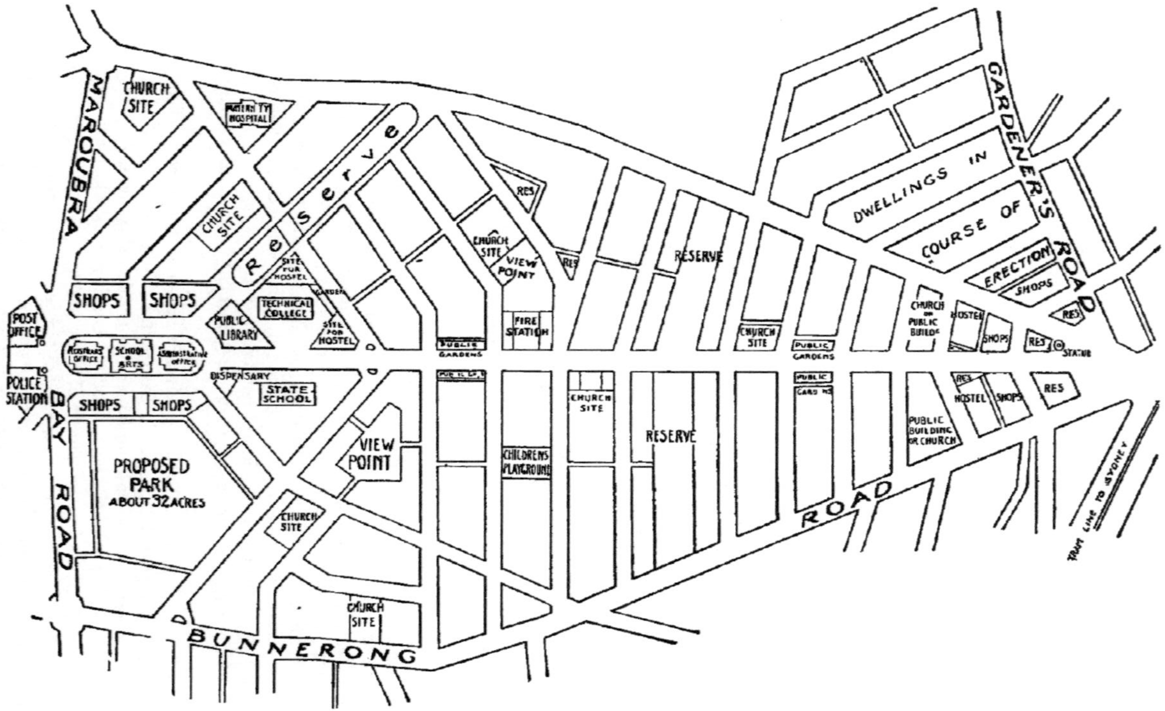

Lay out of the New "Garden Suburb," Daceyville, in Sydney, New South Wales, which is now being developed by the State Housing Board. It will be observed that not only is the lay out open to serious objection, both on the practical and æsthetic sides, but the roads are planned absurdly wide—all 66 feet, in accordance with legislative requirements—and practically the only feature common to Garden Suburbs is that the area is pre-planned!

the villages is Altenhof, designed, as its name suggests, for the old people, pensioners of the firm. There are 600 inhabitants, who live rent free and receive a pension of from £3 to £4 a month. Merely to enumerate the advantages provided for the firm in the way of social and educational advancement, as well as of material benefit, such as savings' banks —where a generous bonus is added to the employees savings—and co-operative societies would occupy more than the whole space devoted to this section. As a social and housing scheme there is nothing in the world in any way comparable to the work at Essen.

Close by, but unconnected with the Krupp colonies, is Margaretenhohe, the "last word" in artistic development and building. The work of an architect who is an artist to his finger tips, promoted by a generous lady who believes in restoring the love of real beauty to a class long divorced therefrom, it is one of those things which no description will do adequate justice to. It should be seen by everybody who wishes to appreciate the possibilities of development which is unstinted in reasonable resources and uncramped by architectural prejudices.

FRANCE.

The French Garden City Association was the first founded outside England, dating from the year 1904, after a visit to Letchworth and the attendance of some meetings by Monsieur Benoit-Levy, who has from that time been the secretary and treasurer of the Association and responsible for the greater part of its activities. Among the founders were Senateur M. d'Estournelles de Constant and Professor Charles Gide, names of world-wide repute.

Although, so far, the Association has not been able to proceed with the work of building on Garden City or Garden Suburb lines, they have influenced the creation of a model mining village of Dourges and have taken an active part in the scheme for the acquisition and preservation of the fortifications This project, which was drawn up by Monsieur Dausset, the general reporter for the Budget of Paris, has been accepted by the Paris Municipality, and now awaits the sanction of Parliament The fortifications, which are of an average of 125 metres wide and are 33 kilometres long, are the property of the State, who have offered them to the City for one hundred million francs. The Association is now organising a campaign in support of purchase.

Largely through Monsieur Levy groups of workers for the Garden City movement have been formed in a number of European cities and assistance has been given in the forming of Associations in other places In Luxemburg, Italy, Roumania, Bohemia, and Turkey, groups have been formed, and it was only the occurrence of the war which prevented the Turkish Association under Niazi Assim Bey being formed. The objects and methods of these various groups, etc., however, are not on all fours with those elsewhere, and it is not easy to determine to what extent the real garden city ideal is advocated.

An enormous amount of literature has been issued, the Association working not only for Garden City ideas properly, but assisting with many other social schemes such as Industrial Welfare, which in England are the affairs of individual associations Monsieur Levy has written a large number of well illustrated books dealing with the Garden City movement, and recently has, in three excellent volumes, dealt with the whole movement with detailed information of the principal schemes in England

AUSTRIA.

Dr Max Ermers (XIX Springsiedelgasse 21, Vienna), well known as a writer upon artistic and architectural subjects, is organising a Garden City Association for Austria and has already gathered round him a number of enthusiastic adherents, many of whom accompanied him last year on a trip of inspection to England. The difficulties to contend with in the country are numerous, but it is hoped that before long active propaganda will be proceeding throughout the empire

BELGIUM.

M Charles Didier, who has for many years carried on the propagandist work in Belgium, acting as secretary to the Belgian Garden City Association, sends the following particulars regarding the movement in his country.—

"The number of people in this country who are interested in Mr. Howard's wonderful conception is infinitely more numerous than one might believe, and that grand social movement, 'The Garden Cities,' is followed intimately and with the greatest sympathy by all those who concern themselves with the great political questions of our day and, above all, of industrial countries like our own

"Unfortunately, I have to make a confession of our lack of success in Belgium On several occasions my friends and I have tried to realise that dream of a Garden City, of a simple Garden Village even, and every time we have failed, but I hasten to add that that failure does not apply in any way to the idea, for everybody, without distinction of party, finds it superb.

"In this country we find ourselves face to face with conditions as to land tenure, etc, which really in a measure make the Garden City unrealisable in Belgium But Mr Howard's idea has none the less a very sensible echo in Belgium, and it has strengthened very much the sense of the absolute necessity of remedying in a definite manner the overcrowding of the towns"

HOLLAND.

Mr. D. de Clercq, of Bloemendaal, who has succeeded Mr Bruyn as the secretary of the Dutch Garden City Association, has during the past few years given a large number of lectures on the Garden City movement and has collected a good deal of literature and a number of lantern slides He has arranged to translate this book into his native language He reports —

"I very much regret to say I cannot give very good news of the movement in Holland We have tried several times to start a society for actual work, but although we have got a few people together, we have not been able to go further It seems that Holland is not yet ready for the movement, the reason being perhaps that we have here only a few big towns, and hundreds of small towns and thousands of villages, with cheap houses and gardens, while the rich people have their country seats quite close to the great towns I have lectured a good many times on the subject and a number of people have taken interest in the movement We intend to continue our lecturing and our propaganda, and by the translation of your books into Dutch, we shall be able to instruct people in the great idea for which you have been responsible."

ITALY.

Several efforts at reformed housing have been made in Italy, but these have been made chiefly upon the old lines of tenement dwellings Near Milan a trial has been made with cottages, and this is said to be upon Garden City lines Repeated application, however, has failed to elicit any information as to whether the scheme is on genuine lines, or is another of the pseudo-garden cities which can be found in practically every European country.

Some German Experiments : 1, Nuremberg ; 2, Margaretenhöhe ; 3, Hellerau.

Nothing could illustrate more vividly the change which the Garden City movement has effected in regard to the question of housing than the above views. The first is a picture of Woodfield Avenue on the estate of the Ealing Tenants Ltd., the first houses erected by the society before it was influenced by the Garden City movement. The second is Fowler's Walk, on the newer portion of the estate.

HUNGARY.

Dr. Elemer Kovats, of VI. Andrassy-ut 60, Budapest, has been responsible for the initiation of a Garden City Association for Hungary, which has decided to issue a periodical dealing with the subject The organisation has only just come into being, but it has considerable promises of support

POLAND.

The Polish Garden City Association was founded by Dr. Dobrzynski in 1909, at Warsaw, and in connection with this a further society was formed, called "The Society for Permanent Dwellings," with the object of preventing speculative building This body has obtained the sanction and approval of the Emperor of Russia. In 1910 an important exhibition was held with the idea of securing support for the movement, and at the end of that year an estate of 210 acres on the Vistula was acquired for the establishment of a Garden Suburb The estate was planned by Mr Bernouilli, an active member of the German Garden City Association, whose work as an architect has won much praise, and architects are now at work on the houses, which will be both detached and in blocks The cheapest house, which will be a two-storey one with four rooms and a garden, will cost 2,600 roubles (about £270) The Association has issued a number of publications and given many lectures A translation has been made of Mr Ebenezer Howard's book *Garden Cities of To-morrow*, and this has had a good circulation in the Russian language. In 1912 a further society was formed called "New Warsaw," with the object of permanently continuing the propaganda. The office of the Association is at Faubourg de Cracovie, 66, Warsaw.

The garden suburb of New Warsaw has been approved by the authorities, and a new electric tram service has been provided to connect the new suburb with the old town. A great deal of good is expected to come from the establishment of this garden suburb, which is primarily due to the devoted labours of Dr. Dobrzynski, one of the founders of the new International Association, and a sincere exponent of Garden City principles. The necessity for the work may be judged from the fact that with a population of 900,000 people, Warsaw possesses only 7,000 houses—one to each 130 people.

RUSSIA.

With M. Dimitri von Protopopoff and M. Alex Bloch as correspondents, a group of workers has been got together in St Petersburg, and it is hoped that practical steps will shortly be taken for the establishment of a Garden Suburb

SPAIN.

A Spanish Garden Cities Association was founded in 1912 by Mr. C. Montoliu, who now acts as Secretary. It bears the name Sociedad Civica La Ciudad Jardin, and has a similar scope to those of other countries In addition to giving many lectures, the Association has taken part in preliminary steps towards the establishment of a Garden Suburb at Barcelona, and has issued many publications, Mr Montoliu having been very active in disseminating information. The registered office of the society is in Barcelona, Calle de Urgel, 187.

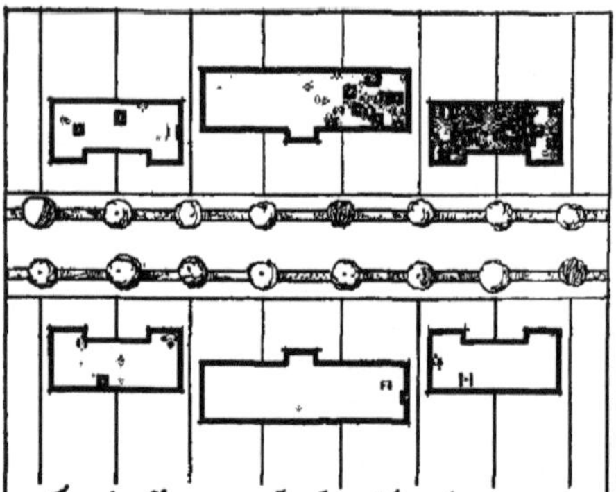

Fig 1. Shewing broken Frontage Line to give Variety.

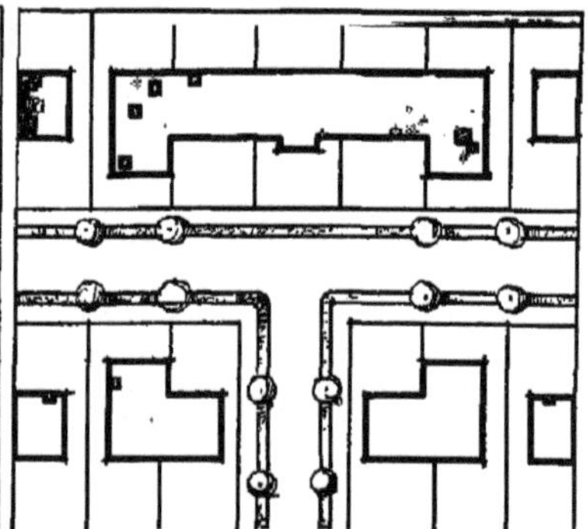

Fig 2. Suggested treatment for Junction of Roads at right angles

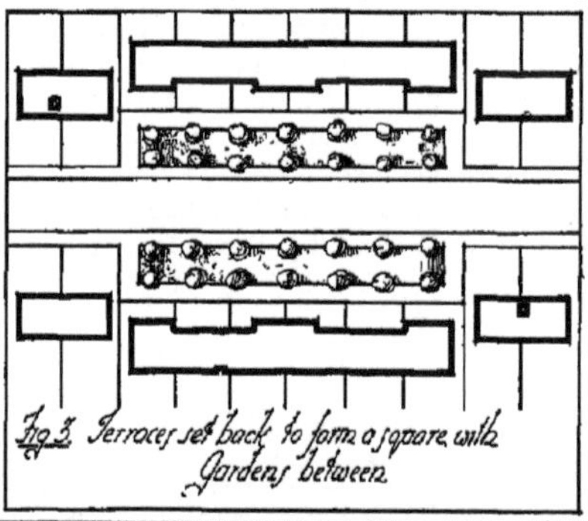

Fig 3. Terraces set back to form a square with Gardens between

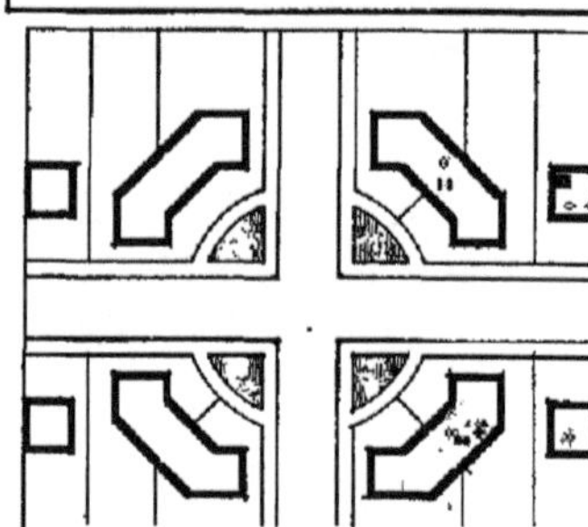

Fig 5. Suggested Intersection

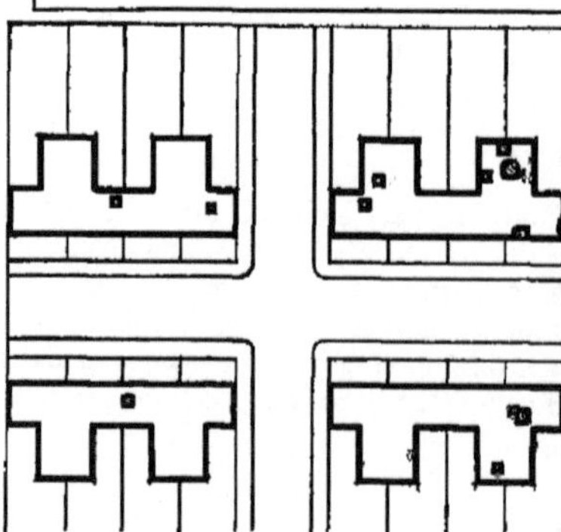

Fig 4 Shewing old method of intersecting

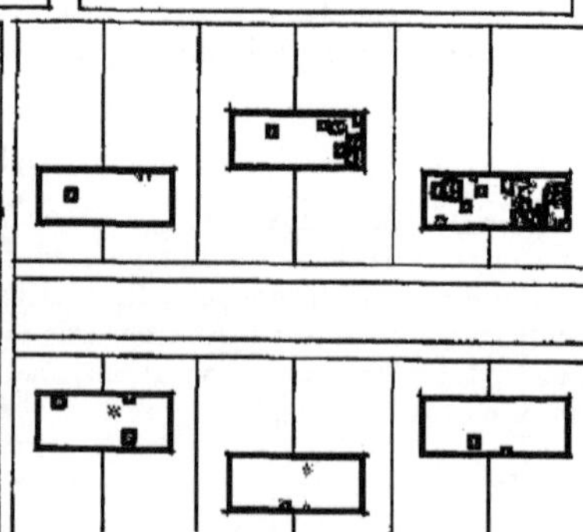

Fig 6 Method of setting semidetached pairs alternately back & forward to secure the

THE INTERNATIONAL GARDEN CITIES AND TOWN PLANNING ASSOCIATION

The International Garden Cities and Town Planning Association was formed on August 22nd, 1913, in order to strengthen the international movement for the extension of the knowledge of the principles laid down by Mr. Ebenezer Howard in his book *Garden Cities of To-morrow.*

President—Mr. Ebenezer Howard.

Chairman—Mr. G. Montagu Harris.

Hon. Secretary—Mr. Ewart G. Culpin.

Offices—3, Gray's Inn Place, Gray's Inn, London, W C

Committee—The Committee consists of representatives of affiliated Societies in the following countries :—

Great Britain	Norway	Hungary
France	Holland	The United States
Germany	Belgium	Canada
Austria	Spain	Australia
Russia	Italy	New Zealand
Poland	Roumania	Japan

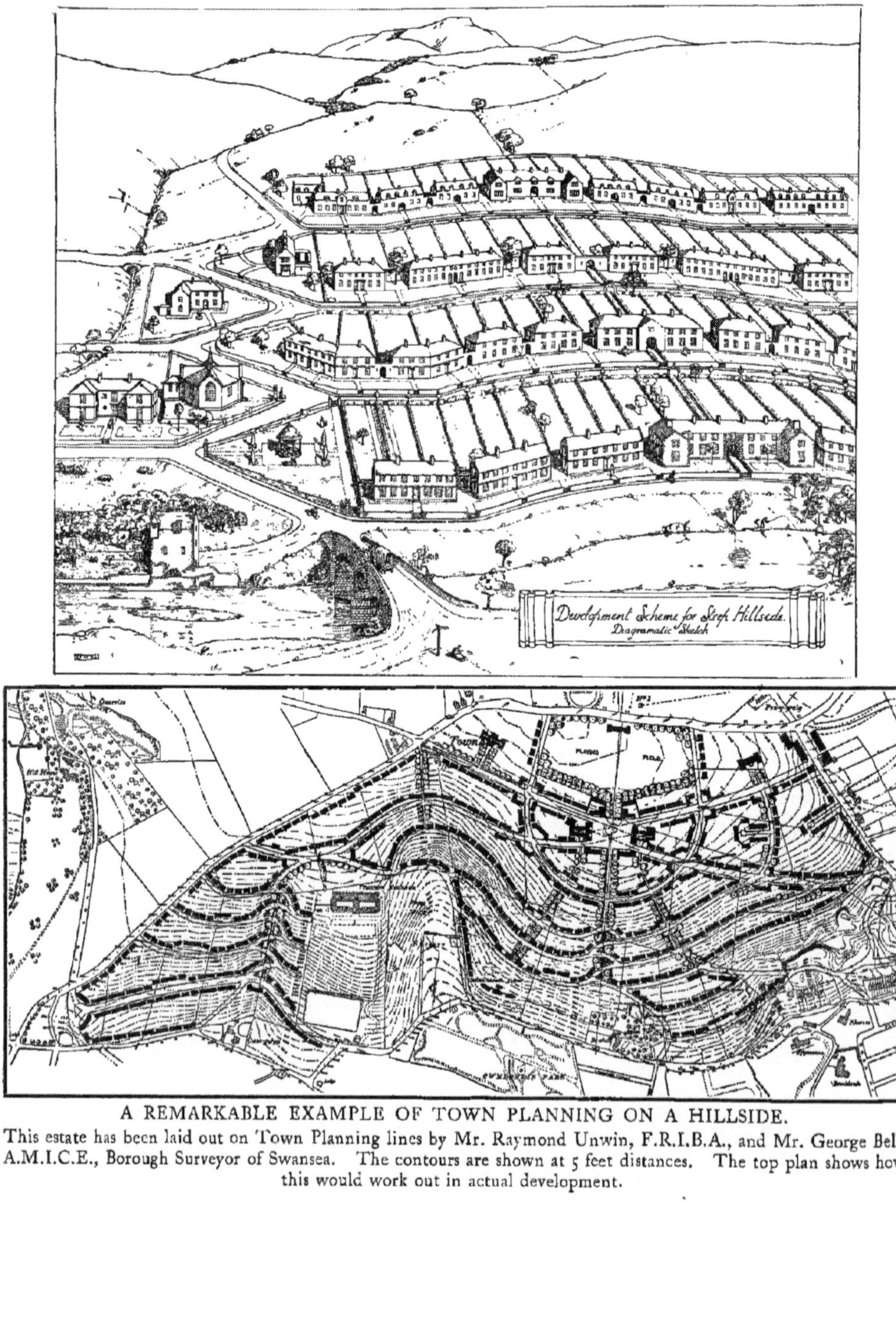

A REMARKABLE EXAMPLE OF TOWN PLANNING ON A HILLSIDE.

This estate has been laid out on Town Planning lines by Mr. Raymond Unwin, F.R.I.B.A., and Mr. George Bell, A.M.I.C.E., Borough Surveyor of Swansea. The contours are shown at 5 feet distances. The top plan shows how this would work out in actual development.

THE GARDEN CITIES AND TOWN PLANNING ASSOCIATION

President—THE HON. MR. JUSTICE NEVILLE
Chairman of Council—CECIL HARMSWORTH, M P
Chairman of Executive—GEORGE L. PEPLER, F S I
Hon Treasurer—FRANCIS E. FREMANTLE, F R C S
Hon Solicitor—HERBERT WARREN.
Hon Auditors—W. B. PEAT & Co.

COUNCIL.

*E. R. ABBOTT.
THOMAS ADAMS.
PROFESSOR S. D. ADSHEAD (Liverpool).
H COLIN ALLEN.
†J H. BARLOW (Bournville).
MRS S. A BARNETT.
*J STANWELL BIRKETT, M A.
†EDGAR L. CHAPPELL (Cardiff)
RT. HON LORD CHARNWOOD (Lichfield)
*†HAROLD CRASKE (First Garden City Ltd)
*†C M CRICKMER, F.R.I.B A.
†WM. DALZIEL (Glasgow).
DAVID DAVIES, M.P.
GEORGE M LL. DAVIES
DR WALTER E LL. DAVIES.
*W. R. DAVIDGE, F.S.I.
*WARWICK H. DRAPER, M.A
†A. E. FRANKLIN (Social Welfare Association)
*FRANCIS E FREMANTLE, F R C S
*†BERNARD GIBSON (M.P.G Assn.)
G P GOOCH, M.A.
H. D. HARBEN.
*G MONTAGU HARRIS, M.A.
*EBENEZER HOWARD
PROFESSOR H. S. JEVONS.
PHILIP T KENWAY
*H. CLAPHAM LANDER, A R I B.A.
†H. J LEANING (London Society).
BRYCE LEICESTER (Liverpool).
†F. LITCHFIELD (Co-partnership Tenants Ltd)
T ALWYN LLOYD.
*R O MOON, M D
REV C. MOOR, D D.
J S. NETTLEFOLD (Birmingham).
MISS E. M NICKOLL
*G. L. PEPLER, F.S I.
ASSHETON POWNALL.
MISS J RECKITT.
†GEORGE ROSE (Liverpool).
†G W ROUSHAM (Hampstead Garden Suburb Trust Ltd)
F. ROWNTREE, F R I.B.A.
†J F. ROXBURGH (Edinburgh).
A. S. SOUTAR, L R I B.A.
RAYMOND UNWIN, F.R.I.B.A.
*F CHILDE WARREN
*HERBERT WARREN
ANEURIN WILLIAMS, M.A
*GLYNNE WILLIAMS
J. FISCHER WILLIAMS.
R. A. YERBURGH, M P.

* *Executive Committee.* † *Representative Member.*

Secretary and Offices—

EWART G. CULPIN.

3, Gray's Inn Place, London, W.C

BRANCH AND AFFILIATED ASSOCIATIONS.

Bolton—W M. FARRINGTON, Borough Hall, Bolton.

East London—J THREADKELL, 17, Clarissa Road, Chadwell Heath.

Edinburgh—GEO. DEAS COWAN, 31, Charlotte Square, Edinburgh.

Glasgow—J. M BIGGAR, 180, West George Street, Glasgow

Letchworth—R. W TABOR, Letchworth

Liverpool—F GRAY WALLIS, 16, Cook Street, Liverpool.

Newcastle-on-Tyne—F. W. SHIELDS, Newcastle.

South Wales—EDGAR L. CHAPPELL, 3, Pembroke Terrace, Cardiff.

Foreign Correspondents.

Austria—DR MAX ERMERS, Glatzgasse 5, Vienna, XIX.

Belgium—CHARLES DIDIER, rue Armand Campenhout, Brussels.

Canada (Halifax)—R M. HATTIE, 27, Coburg Road, Halifax.

Canada (Montreal)—W. H ATHERTON, PH D., City Improvement League, 62, Beaver Hall Hill

Canada (Regina)—R E A LUCK, Secretary, City Planning Association.

France—G BENOIT-LEVY, 11, rue Malebranche, Paris

Germany—ADOLF OTTO, Schlachtensee, bei Berlin

Holland—D DE CLERQ, Bloomendaal

Hungary—DR. ELEMER KOVATS, vi, Andrassy-ut 60, Budapest.

Japan—MR MASAO ITO, Osaka Higher Commercial School, Japan.

Norway—T. SCHLYTTER, Christiania.

Poland—DR DOBRZYNSKI, Faubourg de Cracovie 79, Warsaw.

Roumania—EMIL GUIRGEA, Strade Lueger, 10, Bucharest

Russia—DIMITRI VON PROTOPOPOFF, 14, Kabinetskaja, St. Petersburg.

Spain—M. MONTOLIU, Musee Social, Calle de Urgel, num. 187, Barcelona.

United States—DR. E. E PRATT, 192, Claremont Avenue, New York City

The Garden Cities and Town Planning Association.

CONSTITUTION AND RULES.

I.—Title.

The name of the Association shall be "THE GARDEN CITIES AND TOWN PLANNING ASSOCIATION."

II.—Objects.

The objects of the Association are:—

(*a*) To promote Town Planning
(*b*) To advise on, draw up schemes for, and promote Garden Cities, Garden Suburbs, and Garden Villages.
(*c*) Housing and the improvement of its sanitation.
(*d*) The collection and dissemination of information as to the above.
(*e*) The education of public opinion in these matters.
(*f*) The influencing and promotion of legislation.
(*g*) The improvement of local bye-laws.

III.—Membership.

The Association shall consist of a Central Society and Branches The Central Society shall comprise: (*a*) Honorary Fellows; (*b*) Members; and (*c*) Delegate Members.

Honorary Fellows shall be elected at General Meetings on the nomination of the Council, for services rendered to the ideals of the Association.

Members shall pay a minimum subscription of 5s. per annum

Delegate Members shall be the representatives of Societies approved by the Council, in respect of whose membership such Society shall pay a minimum subscription of 10s 6d, and such members shall be Members of the Council, and shall otherwise have the same powers and rights as ordinary members. Each such Society may send one Delegate Member.

IV.—Management.

1. COUNCIL

(*a*) *Composition*—The management of the Association shall be vested in a Council of not more than fifty members, of whom thirty shall be elected annually The remaining twenty Members shall include *ex-officio* Members, representatives of Branches and Delegate Members, and the Council may at any time fill up any vacancies by co-option.

(*b*) *Election.*—Fourteen days before the Annual General Meeting the Secretary shall send by post to each Member a form inviting nominations for the Council and Officials of the Association. The names so nominated shall be submitted to the Annual General

Meeting for its selection The Council shall elect its own Chairman at its first meeting after the Annual General Meeting.

(*c*) *Meetings*.—The Council shall meet quarterly Special meetings may be called by the Secretary with the authority of the Chairman or on the application of not less than ten Members of the Council Seven shall form a quorum

2 Executive

(*a*) *Appointment*.—At its first meeting after the Annual General Meeting the Council shall elect from its members an Executive Committee of not more than fifteen members.

(*b*) *Powers*.—Subject to the authority of the Council, the Executive Committee shall exercise all powers necessary for the management of the Association, and shall appoint a Finance Committee, and may at its discretion appoint sub-committees, composed either of its own members or other members of the Association, with or without other persons, for the advancement of the purposes enumerated in Rule II, and for any other purposes such as Prospecting and Planning, Legal and Parliamentary, Housing and Public Health, Architecture and Building, Agriculture (including Small Holdings and Allotments), Engineering (Roads, etc), General Purposes and Finance, Women's Organisation Committee, Joint Committees with First Garden City Limited, and similar companies, Foreign Tours, Lectures, and otherwise as it may think fit Casual vacancies shall be filled by co-option.

3 Special Committees.

The Council shall have power to appoint such other Committees as it thinks fit, and to co-opt on such Committees persons who are not Members of the Association.

V.—Officials.

The Association shall have a President, Vice-Presidents and Treasurer, who shall be elected at the Annual General Meeting, or in default thereof, by the Council. The Chairman of the Executive shall be appointed by the Executive The Executive shall be empowered to appoint a Secretary and such other officials as may be necessary

The President and the Honorary Treasurer shall be *ex-officio* Members both of the Council and of the Executive The Chairman of the Council and Executive and the Honorary Treasurer shall be *ex-officio* Members of all Committees

VI.—Branches.

Whenever the Executive thinks fit, and upon the application of residents in any locality, the Association shall recognise a Branch for such locality, if not within the area of any Society already constituted, which should be affiliated to the Association upon the following terms.—

1 That the Branch will subscribe to the principles of the Association as set out in the official handbook, and will undertake to conform to those principles

2 That each Branch shall pay an annual sum to the Association amounting to 20 per cent. of the gross subscriptions, this to entitle the Branch to the following benefits.—

(*a*) A copy of the journal free for each subscriber of 5s, and other literature at trade prices Journals to be supplied in bulk

(*b*) Services of a Lecturer, if required, on the payment of out-of-pocket expenses, and the help and advice of the central organisation.

(*c*) Each Branch shall be entitled to send one representative to act on the Council of the Association, and one Delegate to the General Meeting for any number of members up to 50, two up to 100, and one for each additional 100.

3 The Central Association is not to be debarred from receiving subscriptions direct from any person in the district of the Branch, whether a Member of the Branch or not, and such person subscribing direct to the funds of the Association shall have direct representation, according to General Rules 3 and 4.

4 That the Association will not accept any financial responsibility in respect of any Branch

5. That GARDEN CITIES AND TOWN PLANNING shall be recognised by each Branch as its official organ, to which local information should be supplied

6 No Branch shall be recognised as such until it has received the Certificate of Membership from the Council

7. A copy of the audited accounts, and list of local subscriptions for the previous twelve months shall be sent to the Central Office not later than January 14th each year.

VII.—Accounts.

No accounts shall be paid unless and until they have been authorised or passed by the Finance Committee.

VIII.—Annual General Meeting.

An Annual General Meeting shall be held at such date, hour and place as the Executive may appoint, after giving not less than fourteen days' notice by post to each Member.

IX.—Special General Meeting.

The Council may, at any time, and shall, upon a written requisition sent to the Secretary by Twenty Members, call a Special General Meeting of the Members, giving not less than seven days' notice by post, stating the purposes of the Meeting. At such Meeting fifteen shall form a quorum.

X.—Annual Report.

At the Annual General Meeting a report by the Council on the transactions of the Association and an audited statement of accounts shall be presented for adoption. The report and accounts shall apply to the year ending December 31st.

XI.—Alteration of Rules.

These Rules may be altered at the Annual General Meeting or at any Special General Meeting convened in due form for that purpose. At least fourteen days' notice of any proposed alteration must be given to the Secretary, and such proposed alterations must be set out in the notice convening the meeting.

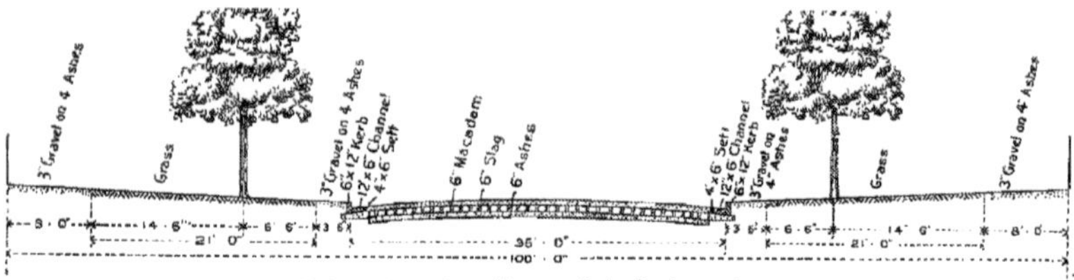

Main road 100 feet wide, metalled only for 35 feet.

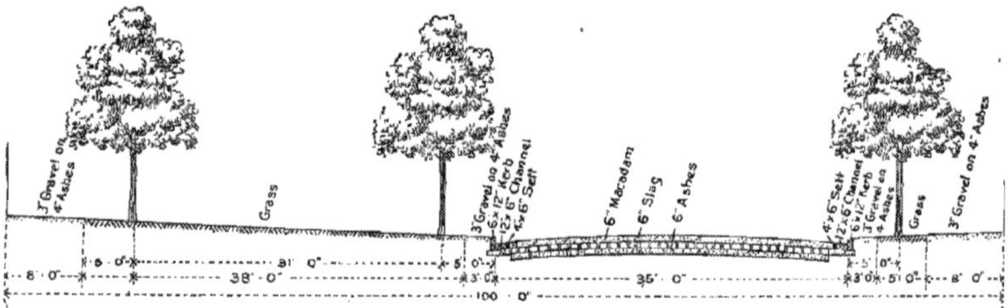

80 feet roadway, with 35 feet metalled and 22 feet devoted to grass margins.

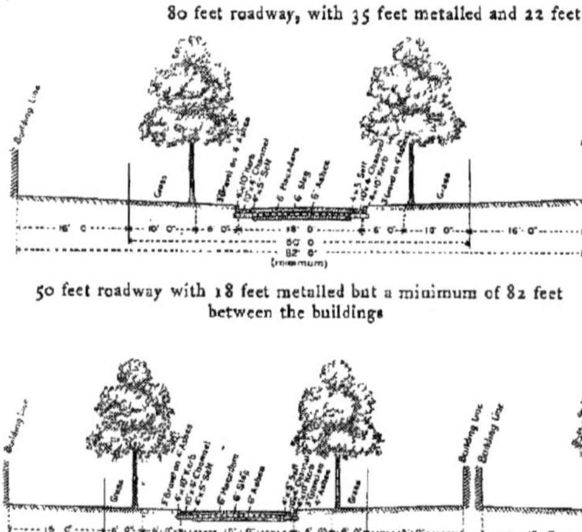

50 feet roadway with 18 feet metalled but a minimum of 82 feet between the buildings

50 feet roadway without grass margins which will be constructed only in the case of widenings to certain existing roads.

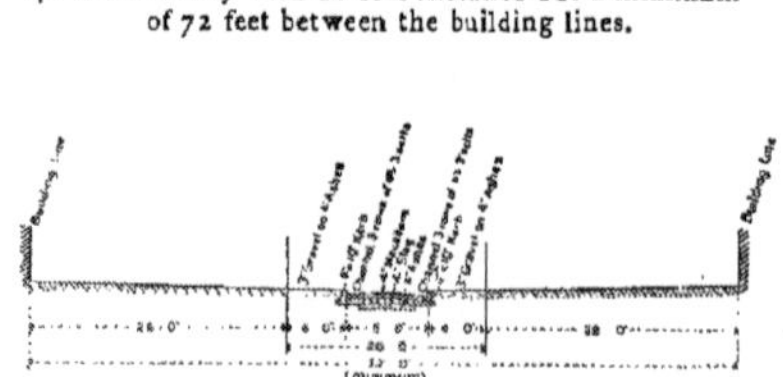

42 feet roadway with 18 feet metalled but a minimum of 72 feet between the building lines.

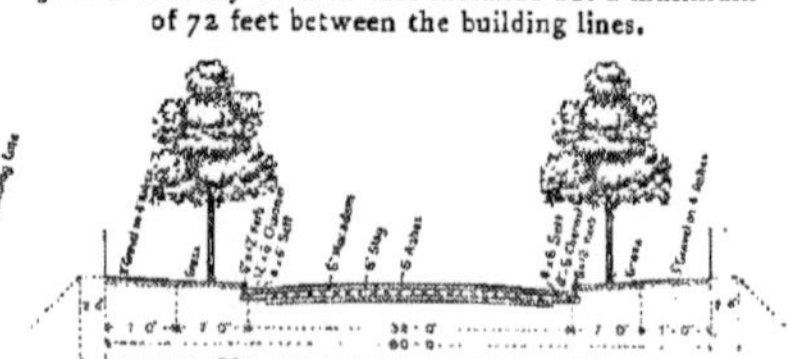

36 feet roadway with 18 feet metalled but a minimum of 72 feet between the building lines.

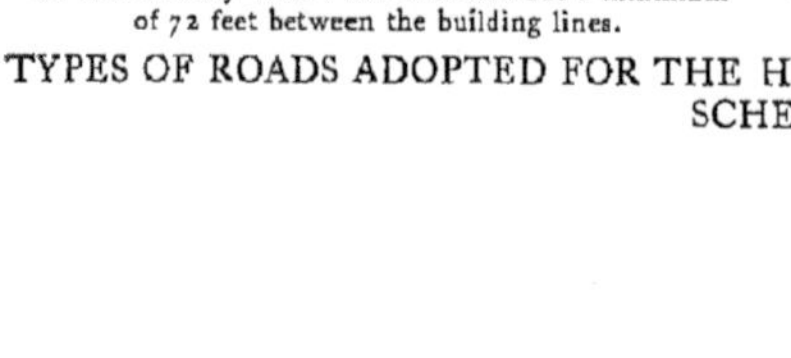

20 feet roadway with 8 feet metalled but a minimum of 72 feet between the building lines.

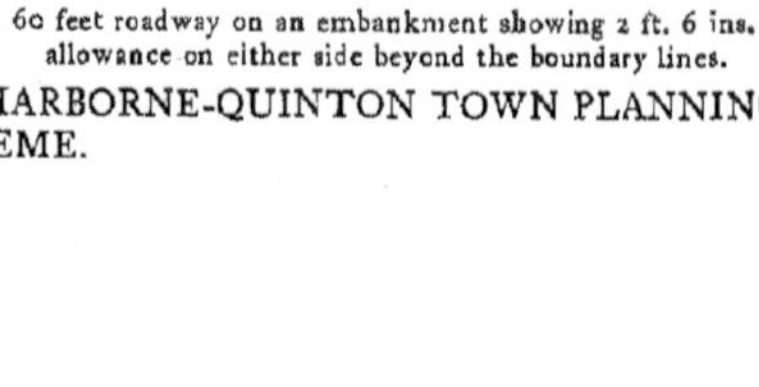

60 feet roadway on an embankment showing 2 ft. 6 ins. allowance on either side beyond the boundary lines.

TYPES OF ROADS ADOPTED FOR THE HARBORNE-QUINTON TOWN PLANNING SCHEME.

The Town Planning Act.

It has been announced that schemes have been prepared by local authorities and submitted to the Local Government Board for approval in the following cases —

Birmingham Corporation —The Quinton, Harborne and Edgbaston Town Planning Schemes relating to an area of about 2,320 acres in the city. (Now finally approved)

Birmingham Corporation —The East Birmingham Town Planning Scheme relating to an area of about 1,442 acres in Aston, in the eastern part of the city.

Rochdale Corporation —The Rochdale Town Planning Scheme (Marland) relating to an area of about 43 acres in the borough

Ruislip-Northwood Urban District Council —An area of about 5,906 acres in the urban district and in the parish of Rickmansworth (rural) in the rural district of Watford.

In the following additional cases the Board are stated to have given authority for the preparation of schemes by local authorities —

Bournemouth Corporation.—An area of about 202 acres in the Boscombe East and Southbourne Wards of the borough.

Bournemouth Corporation.—An area of about 223 acres in the Southbourne Ward of the borough.

Blackburn Corporation.—An area of about 887 acres in the borough and in the rural district of Blackburn.

Carshalton Urban District Council

Cheadle and Gatley Urban District Council.—471 acres.

Chesterfield Corporation —A small area of about 64 acres in the borough

Ellesmere Port and Whitby Urban District Council —An area of about 3,539 acres in the urban district and in the rural district of Chester

Finchley Urban District Council.—An area of about 1,044 acres in the urban district

Halifax Corporation —An area of about 877 acres in the Ovenden and Illingworth Wards of the borough.

Halifax Corporation.—An area of about 749 acres in the Warley, Copley, Illingworth, Ovenden and Pellon Wards of the borough

Hanwell Urban District Council —An area of about 198 acres in the urban district.

Leeds Corporation.—Six acres

Liverpool Corporation —An area of about 88 acres near the eastern boundary of the city.

Liverpool Corporation.—An area of about 1,220 acres in the city and in the urban district of Allerton.

Luton Corporation —An area of about 4,266 acres in the borough and in the rural district of Luton

Much Woolton Urban District Council —An area of about 993 acres in the urban districts of Much Woolton, Little Woolton, and Allerton, and in the rural district of Whiston.

Newcastle-upon-Tyne Corporation —A small area of about 53 acres in the city and in the urban district of Gosforth.

North Bromsgrove Urban District Council.—An area of about 554 acres in the urban district.

Oldbury Urban District Council.—An area of about 1,763 acres in the Warley portion of the urban district

Prestwich Urban District Council.—1,900 acres— Approx 3 sq. miles. City of London is one sq. M.

Richmond (Surrey) Corporation

Scarborough Corporation.—A small area of about 40 acres in the borough

Sheffield Corporation —An area of about 488 acres at Greystones and Bannerdale in the city

Sheffield Corporation —An area of about 97 acres at Sandygate in the city

Sheffield Corporation —An area of about 624 acres at Firth Park, Wincobank and Shire Green in the city.

Southport Corporation —An area of about 2,848 acres in the borough.

Stockport Corporation.

Stoke on-Trent Corporation —An area of about 83 acres in the borough

Sutton Coldfield Corporation —An area of about 6,378 acres in the borough

Twickenham Urban District Council —An area of about 1,860 acres in the urban districts of Twickenham, Heston and Isleworth

Walthamstow Urban District Council —An area of about 1,530 acres in the urban district.

Warrington Corporation —An area of about 1,456 acres in the borough.

Wirral Rural District Council —An area of about 5,742 acres, consisting of the parishes of Great Sutton, Little Sutton, Childer Thornton, Hooton, and Eastham

Wirral Rural District Council —An area of about 3,431 acres, consisting of the parishes of Heswell-cum-Oldfield, Gayton, Pensby, and Barston

Wirral Rural District Council —Two areas of 4,526 acres and 3,013 acres.

Applications for authority to prepare schemes have been made by:—

Hazel Grove and Bramhall Urban District Council

Hunslet Rural District Council.

Halifax No 3 Scheme

Ham Urban District Council

Newton-in-Makerfield Urban District Council

Sheffield Corporation No. 6 Scheme

Bridlington Corporation

Doncaster Rural District Council —Over 5,000 acres.

In the following case the Local Government Board have given authority to a Corporation to adopt with modifications a scheme proposed by owners of land:—

Middleton Corporation.—An area of about 300 acres in the borough

In one case, that of an application from the Corporation of Rochester relating to a very small area, the Board were unable to give the authority asked for as the land was for the most part held by the Secretary of State for War, and being Crown lands could not be included in a town planning scheme.

Preliminary notices have been given under the regulations by the following local authorities with a view to application being made to the Board for authority to prepare schemes, viz —

Acton Urban District Council.
Barnet Valley Urban District Council
Barrow-in-Furness Corporation.
Bristol Corporation.
Chesterfield Corporation.
Doncaster Rural District Council (No 2)
Finchley Urban District Council
Hull Corporation.
Middlesbrough Corporation.
Nelson Corporation.
Shrewsbury Corporation.
Willesden Urban District Council.

It is probable that notices have been given in many other cases.

Other cases in which proposals for schemes are under consideration.—In 31 other cases the Local Government Board reported in November last that information in their possession would seem to indicate that the consideration of the matter by the local authority has reached a stage practically equivalent to a decision to proceed with a scheme Since then other authorities have been reported in the press as taking preliminary steps The following is a list of authorities reported to have proposals for schemes under consideration —

Allerton Urban District Council.
Barnes Urban District Council
Bath Corporation.
Beckenham Urban District Council
Bentley Urban District Council.
Birmingham Corporation —Three areas.
Bolton-upon-Dearne Urban District Council.
Bredbury and Romiley Urban District Council
Caerphilly Urban District Council.
Cheadle and Gatley Urban District Council
Cleckheaton Urban District Council.
Colne Corporation.
Coventry Corporation.
Croydon Corporation
Croydon Rural District Council
Denton Urban District Council
Doncaster Corporation.
Greenford Urban District Council.
Grimsby Rural District Council.
Hailsham Rural District Council
Hendon Urban District Council
Heston Isleworth Urban District Council.
Huddersfield Corporation.

Kingston-upon-Hull Corporation.
Lincoln Corporation.
Little Bebington Urban District Council.
Little Woolton Urban District Council
Maldens (The) and Coombe Urban District Council
Manchester Corporation.
Mansfield Corporation.
Merton Urban District Council.
Mexborough Urban District Council.
Middleton Corporation.
Newcastle-upon-Tyne Corporation.
Otley Urban District Council.
Portsmouth Corporation.
Ripon Corporation.
Rotherham Rural District Council.
Scarborough Corporation.
Sedgley Urban District Council.
Sheffield Corporation
Shoreham-by-Sea Urban District Council
Smethwick Corporation.
Southall-Norwood Urban District Council.
Southgate Urban District Council.
Stockport Corporation.
Stoke-on-Trent Corporation.
Surbiton Urban District Council.
Sutton (Surrey) Urban District Council.
Tynemouth Corporation.
Wallasey Corporation
Wallsend Corporation.
Warrington Rural District Council.
Yeovil Corporation
York Corporation.

In numerous other cases the question of preparing a scheme is under consideration without any definite steps being decided upon, and in this connection the following cases may be mentioned:—

Birkenhead Corporation
Bispham with Norbreck Urban District Council
Bognor Urban District Council.
Bolton Corporation.
Brixham Urban District Council
Buckhurst Hill Urban District Council.
Burnley Corporation.
Bushey Urban District Council.
Christchurch Corporation.

Darfield Urban District Council.
Eastry Rural District Council.
Enfield Urban District Council.
Epsom Rural District Council.
Epsom Urban District Council
Esher and the Dittons Urban District Council
Exeter Corporation.
Gosport and Alverstoke Urban District Council.
Hale Urban District Council.
Harrogate Corporation
Herne Bay Urban District Council.
Hessle Urban District Council.
Irlam Urban District Council.
Leek Urban District Council.
Little Crosby Urban District Council.
Margate Corporation.
Newport (Mon.) Corporation.
Northwich Urban District Council.
Ormesby Urban District Council.
Ossett Corporation.
Rotherham Corporation.
Sidmouth Urban District Council.
Stanley Urban District Council.
Stourbridge Urban District Council.
Stratton and Bude Urban District Council.
Stretford Urban District Council.
Thornton Urban District Council.
Thurnscoe Urban District Council.
Wath-upon-Dearne Urban District Council.
Wakefield Corporation.
Wembley Urban District Council.
Wetherby Rural District Council.
Weymouth Corporation.
Wrexham Corporation.

It will be seen that the names of several local authorities occur in more than one of the foregoing lists, and in these cases the entries refer to different schemes.

There can be little doubt that many other authorities are contemplating town planning schemes. The City of Sheffield alone has ten schemes under consideration.

PLAN OF THE HARBORNE-QUINTON TOWN PLANNING SCHEME AS ADOPTED BY THE BIRMINGHAM CITY COUNCIL

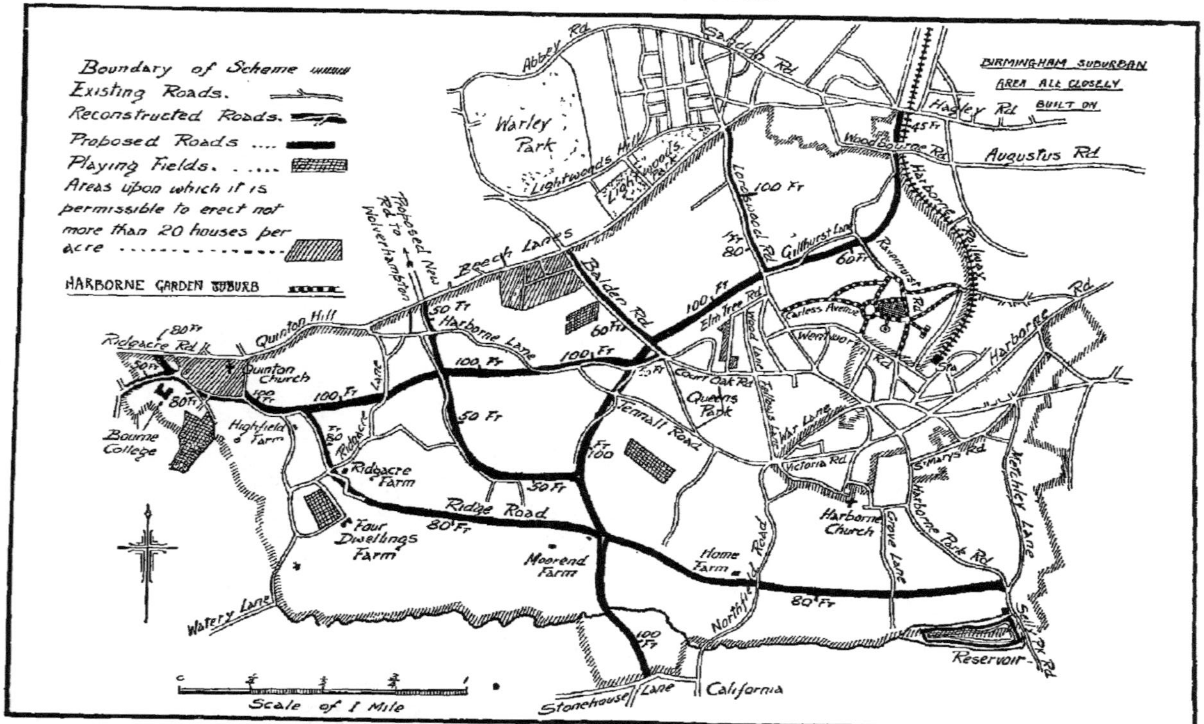

This is the first scheme adopted under the Town Planning Act of 1909. The Harborne Garden Suburb is included in the area.

GARDEN CITY PRESS LIMITED, PRINTERS, LETCHWORTH

Lightning Source UK Ltd.
Milton Keynes UK
UKHW022254240720
367142UK00009B/210

9 780343 005832